PROJECT ACHIEVEMENT:

Reading

George D. Spache, Ph.D.
Spache Educational Consultants

Evelyn B. Spache, Ed.D.
Spache Educational Consultants

And the Scholastic Editors

B

 **Scholastic Book Services**
New York Toronto London Auckland Sydney Tokyo

The Project Achievement Staff

Curriculum Consultant: Leonore K. Itzkowitz, Reading Specialist, New Jersey Public Schools
Editors: Michael E. Goodman, Doreen Nation, Lucy Straus
Editorial Director: Eleanor Angeles

Production Editor: Karen Bergen
Senior Art Director: Mary Mars
Senior Designer: Marijka Kostiw

Design: Taurins Design Associates
Photo Research: Sybille Millard

Art Credits: Andrea Baruffi, pp. 38, 39, 52, 81, 89, 115, 130 • Doron Ben-Ami, pp. 68 • Llynne Buschman, pp. 18, 19, 82 • Bradley Hales Clark, pp. 32, 60, 61, 100, 101 • Cynthia Watts Clark, pp. 37, 80, 128 • Marita Susan Faiola, pp. 41, 44, 84, 85, 103 • Shelly Freshman, pp. 36, 141, 142 • Heather Gilchrist, p. 94 • Donna Ruff, pp. 105, 137 • David Tamura, pp. 12, 30 • U.S. Patent Office, Dover, NY/1970, p. 102

Cover Illustration: Jeanette Adams
Cover Photo: Courtesy of The Port Authority of NY and NJ

Photo Credits: Courtesy of The Port Authority of NY and NJ, p. 5 • Scholastic Awards/Jay David Blumenfeld, p. 7; Paul Paoli, p. 47; Randy Wright, p. 79; Randall Maxwell, p. 149; Jon Clarke Martin, p. 197 • New York Times Pictures/Arlen Pennell, p. 9 • John Sotomayor, p. 57 • Courtesy of N.Y. Convention and Visitors Bureau, p. 10 • United Press International, pp. 15, 29, 43, 54, 107 • Howard Millard, p. 17 • Fred Lyon, p. 21 • Photo Researchers, Inc./Jerome Wexler, p. 22 • Courtesy of ABC Television Network, pp. 35, 146 • Jack George Tauss, p. 51 • Time Magazine/Ted Thai, p. 58 • Wide World Photo, Inc., pp. 62, 75, 134 • Courtesy of American Lung Association, p. 65 • Julie Jensen, p. 67 • Rosica, Mulhern Associates, Inc., p. 71 • U.S. Geological Survey, Department of the Interior, p. 73 • Martha Ledger, p. 91 • Newsweek/Bernard Gotfryd, p. 97 • Courtesy of Museum of Modern Art/Film Stills Archive, p. 112 • Courtesy of Toshiko d'Elia, p. 118 • Courtesy of the Swiss National Tourist Office, p. 140 • Archive Pictures, Inc/Charles Harbutt, p. 140 • James Gilmour, pp. 174, 175, 188, 192, 193, 217

Grateful acknowledgement is made to the following authors and publishers for the use of copyrighted materials. Every effort has been made to obtain permission to use previously published material. Any errors or omissions are unintentional.

Atheneum Publishers for "Night," ("A Wolf . . .,") Osage poem from SONGS OF THE DREAM PEOPLE: CHANTS AND IMAGES FROM THE INDIANS AND ESKIMOS OF NORTH AMERICA. Edited by James Houston. Copyright © 1972 by James Houston, A Margaret K. McElderry Book.

Cold Mountain Press for "Birdfoot's Grampa" by Joseph Bruchac from ENTERING ONANDAGA. Copyright © 1975 by Joseph Bruchac.

Doubleday & Co. Inc. for "The Bat" from THE COLLECTED POEMS OF THEODORE ROETHKE. Copyright 1938 by Theodore Roethke.

M. Evans Brothers Ltd. for "The Fog" by F.R. McCreary from FRANC FANCY FREE.

Macmillan Publishing Co., Inc. for "The Seagull Curves His Wings" from SUMMER GREEN by Elizabeth Coatsworth. Copyright 1947 by Macmillan Publishing Co., Inc. Copyright renewed 1975 by Elizabeth Coatsworth Beston.

ISBN 0-590-34244-4

12 11 10 9 8 7 6 5 4 3 2 1   9   2 3 4 5 6/8
09

Contents

4

Introduction

How does anyone learn to read well? There is no secret about becoming a good reader. Good reading takes practice. You can learn to read well by practicing four different ways:

1. By following the ideas in a story.

Here is a part of a story you will find in this book.

The George Washington Bridge opened in 1931. This bridge connects New York and New Jersey. Before the bridge was built, people took a ferry boat across the water. The bridge helped the area to expand quickly. Soon many people moved into the growing area.

Nearly 260 people now work on the bridge. They have seen some extraordinary events. One time an airplane landed on the bridge. Another time a truck filled with watermelons turned over. Once a long truck nearly drove off the bridge. The driver was suspended over the water, but he was soon rescued.

Finish the sentence. The George Washington Bridge is between New York and __.

2. By figuring out what new words mean.

The words under **A** are from the story above.
Match each word with its meaning under **B**.

A	B
expand	unusual
extraordinary	hanging
suspended	grow

Find two more ways to read well on the next page.

3. By using lists of facts and other visual materials.

Use the table to answer the question below.

THE LONGEST SUSPENSION BRIDGES IN NORTH AMERICA

Bridge	Place	Length
Verrazano-Narrows	New York City	4,260 feet
Golden Gate	San Francisco	4,200 feet
Mackinac	Mackinaw City, MI	3,800 feet
George Washington	New York City	3,500 feet
Tacoma	Tacoma, WA	2,800 feet

What is the longest bridge under 4,000 feet? __

4. By knowing how to take reading tests.

Building a bridge can be dangerous work. It took four years to build the Golden Gate Bridge in San Francisco. Workers climbed hundreds of feet above the icy water. A net was hung under the bridge to catch any workers who might fall.

Choose the best answer.

This paragraph is mostly about __.
   a. driving on the Golden Gate Bridge
   b. the longest bridges
   c. building the Golden Gate Bridge
   d. climbing the hills of San Francisco

Now you have practiced four kinds of reading skills. You will find the same kinds of skills in the rest of this book.

Answers to exercises: 1. New Jersey, **2.** expand-grow, extraordinary-unusual, suspended-hanging, **3.** Mackinac, **4.** c

UNIT I
READING COMPREHENSION

Details are the small parts in a whole thing. The picture on page 8 has many details. It shows a robot and the man who built it. Study the details in the picture. Then answer the following questions.

Choose the best answer for each question.

1. The man is using a tool to fix the robot's ___.
   a. head
   b. arm
   c. light

Check your answer. The robot has a shape a little like the human body, and the part being fixed is its arm. The answer is **b**.

2. At the top end of the robot's arm is ___.
   a. a wrench for holding things
   b. a wire for tying things
   c. a tool for opening things

Check your answer. The top end of the robot's arm is a wrench. The answer is **a**.

3. Where are the buttons to control the robot?
   a. on the arm
   b. on top of the head
   c. on the front

Check your answer. Notice the panel of buttons on the front of the robot. The right answer is **c**.

4. The robot is built to move on ___.
   a. two feet
   b. a round base
   c. four metal cups

Check your answer. The bottom part of the robot is a round base. The answer is **b**.

5. How tall is the robot, compared to the man?
   a. taller than the man
   b. about the same height as the man
   c. much shorter than the man

Check your answer. The robot is on a table. That makes it seem taller than it really is. The answer is **c**.

LESSON 1

Details are the small facts in a story. Read this story and look for the details. Finding details will help you understand what you read.

The Longest Street

The longest city street in the world is in Los Angeles. It is called Figueroa Street. The street was named after José Figueroa, a governor of Mexico at one time.

Figueroa Street runs north and south through Los Angeles for a distance of 30 miles. It connects Pasadena in the north to San Pedro in the south. It is the only street in the world that runs 30 miles through the same city.

Another long city street is Broadway, in New York City. Broadway is 16 miles long inside the city. The street continues north outside the city for another 140 miles. It keeps the name of Broadway, but it passes through many other cities and towns.

The photo shows Broadway in New York City.

Choose the best answer for each question.

1. Where is Figueroa Street?
  a. in Los Angeles
  b. in Mexico
  c. in New York City

Check your answer. Notice the word *where* in the question. The answer will be the name of a place. Find the *right* place by looking back at the story. The answer is **a**.

2. How long is Figueroa Street?
  a. 16 miles
  b. 30 miles
  c. 140 miles

Check your answer. Look for the right number to answer the question. Don't be fooled by other numbers in the story. The right answer is **b**.

3. Who was José Figueroa?
  a. a person from Los Angeles
  b. a governor of Mexico
  c. a president of the U.S.

Check your answer. Find the name *José Figueroa* in the story. Look for the right detail in the same sentence. The answer is **b**.

4. The city at the north end of Figueroa Street is ___.
  a. Los Angeles
  b. San Pedro
  c. Pasadena

Check your answer. Find the word *north* in the story. Look for the name of the city that is north. The right answer is **c**.

5. How much longer is Figueroa Street than Broadway, in New York City?
  a. 14 miles
  b. 16 miles
  c. 30 miles

Check your answer. You must subtract 16 from 30 to find the answer. The answer is **a**.

Details in this story are about things that happened in an accident. Read the story and look for these details.

Too Much Water

Flooded roads are dangerous for drivers. In the summer of 1981, heavy rain caused flooding on a main road in New Jersey. Four trucks crashed because of the flooding.

The accident happened at 2:30 a.m. It started when a truck slowed down in the right lane because of deep water on the road. A second truck came up close behind it. The driver was not able to stop in time and hit the first truck in the rear. The third truck, a newspaper delivery truck, skidded on the wet road and hit the second truck. The driver of the fourth truck tried to pull into the left lane but could not keep from crashing into the other trucks.

One of the trucks was carrying a load of fish. Part of the load spilled and ended up on the highway.

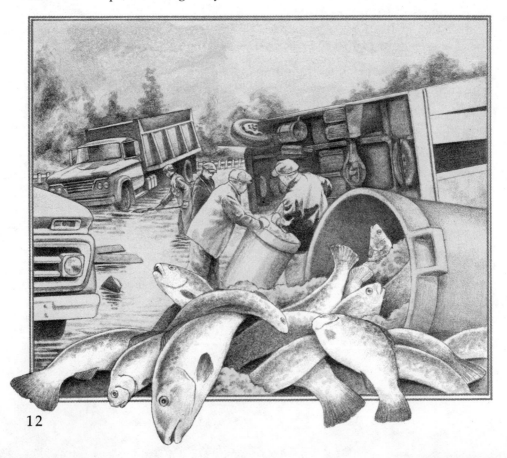

Choose the best answer for each question.

1. When did the accident happen?
   a. in late morning
   b. in the afternoon
   c. in the middle of the night

2. What happened first in the accident?
   a. A truck slowed down.
   b. A load of fish spilled.
   c. Four trucks crashed.

3. The cause of the accident seemed to be ___.
   a. too many trucks
   b. water on the road
   c. fish on the road

4. What was the third truck carrying?
   a. newspapers
   b. fish
   c. bottles of water

5. The driver of the fourth truck tried to ___.
   a. stop on the road
   b. take another road
   c. pull away from the other trucks

Check your answers.

Question 1: The story says that 2:30 a.m. was the time of the accident. That is in the middle of the night. The answer is **c**.

Question 2: The story tells how the accident started. Find the right details. The answer is **a**.

Question 3: The question asks about a *cause*. Look for a sentence with the word *because*. Then choose the best answer. The answer is **b**.

Question 4: There are details in the story about four trucks. Find the details about the third truck. The right answer is **a**.

Question 5: Look for details about the fourth truck. The details would come near the end of the story. The answer is **c**.

Practice finding details in the next stories. Look back at the stories to answer the questions.

___

The House That Was Never Finished

Sarah Winchester was a very rich woman. She didn't buy many jewels or fancy clothes. Instead, she spent millions of dollars to build a house. The strange thing about Sarah's house was that it was never finished. Work on the house went on for 38 years because Sarah was afraid to stop building it.

Sarah's house was near San Jose, California. Every day, a crew of carpenters, plumbers, and other workers arrived there. Sarah wanted more rooms and more doors and windows, so the workers kept on building them. The house was seven floors high and had 160 rooms. There were 2,000 doors and 10,000 windows. There were also three elevators, nine kitchens, and 47 fireplaces.

Why did Sarah want a house that kept getting bigger? The reason seemed to be that Sarah was afraid of dying. She thought she would die when the house was finished, so she made certain that it was never finished.

Sarah Winchester's plan seemed to have worked because she lived to be 83 years old. Finally, her house was finished.

___

Choose the best answer for each question.

1. Where did Sarah Winchester live?
   a. near San Antonio
   b. near San Jose
   c. near San Francisco

2. What did Sarah keep doing to her house?
   a. making it cleaner
   b. making it quieter
   c. making it bigger

3. The story says that Sarah's house had __.
   a. 7 floors
   b. 40 floors
   c. 160 floors

4. Who did the work on Sarah's house?
   a. Sarah herself
   b. Sarah's children
   c. carpenters and plumbers

5. How long did the work on the house continue?
   a. for 7 years
   b. for 38 years
   c. for 83 years

6. Sarah's house was finally finished ___.
   a. when she moved in
   b. when she spent all her money
   c. when she died

Stay in Shape

If you want to be healthy, you must stay in good shape. The best way to stay in shape is to do aerobic exercises. These exercises give your heart and lungs a good workout. If your heart and lungs are strong, your blood will flow better. Your muscles will be stronger. You will look better and feel better.

Some good aerobic exercises are jogging, running, swimming, dancing, skipping rope, and even walking. Good aerobic sports are basketball, soccer, rowing, and skating.

You must train your body to do the exercises. You should build up the exercises slowly. You should also take time to warm up before you exercise, and to cool down afterward. Otherwise, you might strain your muscles.

Here are some ways to warm up. Bend to the side. Bend your knees. Touch your toes. Stretch your calf muscles by putting one heel behind you. Then lean forward until you feel your calf muscle pulling. To stretch your thigh muscles, bend one knee a little. Then slide the other leg straight out. Work up to holding your leg out for 25–30 seconds. Then switch legs.

After your body is warm, exercise for 25–30 minutes. You can even do aerobics inside. Turn on your favorite music. Then run, jump, or dance to the music. Get all of your body moving. Keep up a strong, steady pace. Try to breathe deeply while you exercise.

Afterward, cool down by moving slowly. Sway from side to side, circle your arms, and lift your knees high. Stretch your leg muscles again. Then relax.

Choose the best answer for each question.

1. Aerobic exercises can make your muscles ___.
   a. larger
   b. tighter
   c. stronger

2. Two aerobic exercises are ___.
   a. baseball and rowing
   b. jogging and dancing
   c. walking and hopping

3. The first step in aerobic exercises is to ___.
   a. warm up
   b. cool down
   c. jump to music

4. How do you stretch the thigh muscles?
   a. bend to the side
   b. bend one knee
   c. lean forward

5. You should do aerobic exercises for ___.
   a. 25–30 seconds
   b. 10–15 minutes
   c. 25–30 minutes

6. To *cool down* means to ___.
   a. dance to music
   b. move slower little by little
   c. touch the toes

LESSON 5

Good Luck, Bad Luck

Will you have good luck if you carry a silver dollar? Many people believe that carrying a certain coin can bring good luck. Sometimes women wear a coin on a bracelet for luck.

A coin with a hole in it is supposed to be especially lucky in some countries. This idea got started long ago, before coins were used. People believed that a shell or a stone with a hole in it could keep away evil spirits. Coins with a hole would do the same.

There are many other beliefs about how money can bring good luck. Here are a few examples. If you find a coin, you will find even more coins. A jar of pennies in the kitchen will bring good luck. A coin in the bride's shoe at a wedding will lead to a happy marriage. If you give a wallet or a purse as a present, put a coin inside. Then the new owner will never be without money.

There are also stories about how money may bring bad luck. One story says that it is unlucky to dream about money. Another story warns about what may happen when you carry coins in a pocket. Shaking the coins and making jangling noises will bring bad luck in love.

Choose the best answer for each question.

1. What kind of coin is supposed to keep away evil spirits?
 a. a round coin
 b. a coin with a hole in it
 c. a heavy coin

2. What is supposed to happen if you find a coin?
 a. You will lose the coin.
 b. You will dream about the coin.
 c. You will find more coins.

3. A coin in a bride's shoe is supposed to lead to __.
 a. more coins
 b. bad luck
 c. a happy marriage

4. Which of these is supposed to bring bad luck?
 a. dreaming about money
 b. a jar of pennies
 c. a silver dollar

5. Shaking a pocketful of coins is supposed to bring __.
 a. good luck
 b. bad luck
 c. more coins

6. Most of the details in the story are about __.
 a. how coins bring good luck
 b. how coins bring bad luck
 c. silver dollars

The Birds with Red Heads

It is not easy to fool a scientist. But even scientists get fooled once in a while. That is what happened in San Francisco one year.

San Francisco is a city on a bay. Sea gulls fly low over the water to look for food. In 1935, some strange-looking birds began appearing over the bay. These birds were gray and white with large wings, and looked almost exactly like sea gulls. One thing was different about these birds. They had red heads. Until then, nobody had ever seen a red-headed sea gull.

News about the red-headed birds spread quickly. Scientists came to study the birds and take pictures. They wrote articles about this new kind of bird. Then the scientists realized that they had been fooled. The true story about the red-headed birds came out.

The birds were really plain sea gulls after all. They got their red heads because they were hungry. In 1935, the new Golden Gate Bridge was being built in San Francisco. Workers were painting the bridge and took their lunch hour up there. Sea gulls flew close by to beg for food. They came so close that the workers had a contest. Who could do the best job of dabbing red paint on the heads of the sea gulls?

That is how the red-headed sea gulls came to San Francisco.

Choose the best answer for each question.

1. San Francisco is near a __.
   a. mountain
   b. desert
   c. body of water

2. The colors of a sea gull are __.
   a. gray and white
   b. red and white
   c. gray and red

3. At first, the scientists thought they had seen __.
   a. a new bridge
   b. a new kind of bird
   c. a small sea gull

4. What did the scientists do?
   a. They chased the birds.
   b. They fed the birds.
   c. They took pictures of the birds.

5. What were the workers doing on the Golden Gate Bridge?
   a. building the bridge
   b. painting the bridge
   c. fixing the bridge

6. The sea gulls came close to the bridge because ___.
   a. they were hungry
   b. they were tired
   c. they were wet

Plants That Eat Animals

Many people are always looking for the best plant food to help their plants to grow. Some plants don't need to be fed. They can catch their own food as it flies by. Here is how it happens.

A fly buzzes around a small green plant. The plant's open leaves are bright red in the middle. The leaves have a sweet smell. The fly lands on the leaves to get food. Before the fly can eat, the leaves snap shut. The fly is trapped inside. The Venus flytrap has caught its supper.

Juices in the leaves break down the fly's body and change it into bits of food. Slowly, the leaves take in the food. In a few days, the leaves open wide again. There is no sign that a fly has been trapped and eaten. The Venus flytrap is ready for its next meal.

The Venus flytrap is not the only plant that eats meat. The sundew and the pitcher plant are two other meat-eaters. No meat-eating plants eat anything very big. There have been stories about trees in Africa that eat people, but these stories are not true. The biggest animal that a meat-eating plant can eat is a tiny frog.

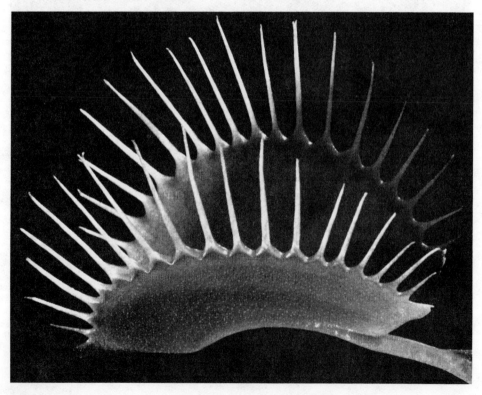

Choose the best answer for each question.

1. The leaves of a Venus flytrap have __.
   a. a sweet smell
   b. a sour smell
   c. no smell

2. What color is a Venus flytrap?
   a. all green
   b. green and red
   c. bright red

3. What happens after a fly lands on the leaves?
   a. The leaves get smaller.
   b. The leaves snap shut.
   c. The fly gets food.

4. Juices in the leaves __.
   a. change the fly into food
   b. make the fly bigger
   c. help the fly to swim

5. Meat-eating plants eat only animals that are __.
   a. green
   b. slow
   c. tiny

6. How many kinds of plants eat meat?
   a. only one
   b. only two
   c. at least three

TAKING TESTS

Practice finding details in a reading passage. Follow the test tips on the next four pages. Put your answers on your answer sheet.

Test Tips: On most reading tests, each question has four answers below it. Read all the answers to a question before you choose the best one.

Stamp collecting is popular all over the world. Every country uses stamps, and many people collect them. In the U.S. alone, about 24 million people collect stamps.

Stamp collecting began in 1840. The first stamp was sold in England that year. It showed a picture of Queen Victoria. Now there are more than 300,000 kinds of stamps. Collectors cannot get every kind of stamp ever made. Instead, people often save stamps on one subject, such as sports or birds. Some people save stamps from one country.

Stamps can make money for a collector. Like coins, stamps are worth more as they get older. The first stamp from England is worth a few thousand dollars now. Stamps can also be worth a lot because of a printing mistake. A 1918 U.S. airmail stamp is worth more than $70,000 now because the airplane on it was printed upside down.

---

1. How many stamp collectors are in the U.S.?
   a. about 24,000
   b. about 70,000
   c. about 300,000
   d. about 24 million

2. Where was the first stamp printed?
   a. the U.S.   c. China
   b. England   d. Canada

3. A stamp from 1840 showed a picture of __.
   a. birds
   b. an airplane
   c. Queen Victoria
   d. a sports team

4. As stamps get older, they are __.
   a. worth more
   b. worth less
   c. not for sale
   d. black and white

5. A mistake on a 1918 stamp showed __.
   a. an airplane landing
   b. an airplane upside down
   c. two airplanes
   d. the wrong airplane

Test Tips: On a test, answer all the questions you are sure of first. Then go back to the others. Put a mark beside the ones you skipped.

Imagine walking to your car in a parking lot. Suddenly you see two alligators chasing each other. That sight might surprise you. But many people in Florida and Louisiana have gotten used to seeing alligators everywhere.

The problem with alligators began after 1967. Before then, hunters killed alligators by the thousands. Their skins were turned into shoes and handbags.

Then some people began to worry that every single alligator would be killed. So in 1967, a new law put an end to alligator hunting. Soon the number of alligators grew much larger. There were half a million alligators in Florida alone. They were not afraid to crawl near people. They showed up on streets and parking lots, and even in swimming pools.

There were so many alligators that the law had to be changed. Now hunters are allowed to go after the alligators again. The change in the law has made some people angry. They want to protect the alligators. But other people are happy to keep the alligators away from their homes and families.

---

1. Alligator skins have been used to make __.
   a. shoes and socks
   b. shoes and handbags
   c. handbags and hats
   d. handbags and socks

2. In 1967, a new law put an end to __.
   a. petting alligators
   b. feeding alligators
   c. hunting alligators
   d. walking alligators

3. How many alligators were in Florida soon after 1967?
   a. 500   c. half a million
   b. 1,000   d. one million

4. The article says that alligators were found in __.
   a. pools
   b. stores
   c. shoes
   d. schools

5. Which of the following is true about alligators?
   a. They stay away from people.
   b. They are getting smaller.
   c. They sleep under cars.
   d. They live in Louisiana.

TAKING TESTS

Test Tips: Try reading the questions before you read the story. Then you will know what details to look for. Read the questions now. Then read the story.

Fires start in many ways. Some fires start by accident when people are not careful. Other fires are caused by nature, as when lightning strikes a tree. Perhaps the most terrible cause of fire is arson.

Arson is setting a fire on purpose to do harm. Every year in the U.S., 1,000 people die because of arson. Another 10,000 people are hurt. Arson is the most costly crime there is.

Why do people set fires on purpose? Often they burn their own houses or buildings to get insurance money. Some people set fires because they are angry at someone and want to "get even." Others start fires just because they like to watch things burn.

Arson can do harm in other ways besides killing people. In November, 1981, someone set a fire on purpose in Lynn, Massachusetts. The fire did $40 million worth of damage. Hundreds of old people lost their homes. About 1,500 people lost their jobs because their factories burned.

Police and fire fighters are working together to stop arson. At each fire, they look for clues about the cause of the fire. They are also teaching people about arson and how it can harm others.

---

1. What is arson?
   a. starting a fight
   b. stealing money from a bank
   c. starting a fire to do harm
   d. killing a person

2. How many people in the U.S. die each year because of arson?
   a. 100   c. 10,000
   b. 1,000   d. 100,000

3. Why do some people burn their own houses?
   a. to make the house darker
   b. to get even with themselves
   c. to make the house warmer
   d. to get insurance money

4. Many people lost their jobs in Lynn because __.
   a. their factories burned
   b. they did poor work
   c. they were too old
   d. they set a fire together

5. At each fire, police and fire fighters __.
   a. work all night
   b. look for clues
   c. wait for lightning
   d. build a factory

Test Tips: Notice dates and other numbers in a reading passage. Be prepared to answer questions about them.

___

In 1963, workers began to build a new stadium in Houston, Texas. It was to be for baseball and football games. This would be no ordinary stadium. This stadium was going to have a roof.

Many people laughed when they heard about the plan. No field that big had a roof over it. People said the roof would cave in. But two years later, the Astrodome was finished. The roof was in place.

The Astrodome is an amazing piece of work. Eight hundred workers were needed for the job. The stadium covers nine acres of land. The roof is 208 feet high—as high as an 18-story building. Inside, there are 50,000 seats, plus a two-million-dollar scoreboard and a giant air conditioner. Games can be played in any kind of weather.

At first, the Astrodome had a field of real grass. As the grass grew, it sent moisture into the air. The air inside the stadium got wetter and wetter. The grass had to be taken out. Fake grass, called Astroturf, replaced the real grass.

The Astrodome is now used for more than baseball and football games. People go there to see the circus, car races, boxing, and even bullfights.

___

1. How long did it take to build the Astrodome?
   a. a year   c. five years
   b. two years   d. nine years

2. Some people thought the roof would ___.
   a. get too hot
   b. kill the grass
   c. cave in
   d. be too low

3. How many people can sit in the Astrodome?
   a. 800   c. 100,000
   b. 50,000   d. 2 million

4. How high is the roof of the Astrodome?
   a. 208 feet
   b. 500 feet
   c. 1,800 feet
   d. 2,080 feet

5. Astroturf is used on the ___.
   a. roof
   b. scoreboard
   c. seats
   d. field

Study the picture of the marchers on page 28. What is the picture about? What is the main idea? To find the main idea, add up the details. The questions below will help you to find the main idea.

Choose the best answer for each question.

1. The marchers are all wearing ___.
   a. uniforms of long ago
   b. everyday clothes
   c. baseball uniforms

Check your answer. Look at the clothes of the marchers. Then choose the right detail. The answer is **a**.

2. What kinds of musical instruments are shown?
   a. horns and bells
   b. drums and trumpets
   c. drums and flutes

Check your answer. The marchers are playing drums and flutes. The right answer is **c**.

3. All of the marchers are ___.
   a. running in place
   b. marching in step
   c. carrying musical instruments

Check your answer. Did you notice that the marcher at the right is not carrying a musical instrument? The right answer has to be **b**.

4. Where are the marchers headed?
   a. across a field
   b. along a city street
   c. into a stadium

Check your answer. Notice the pavement, and the city buildings in the background. The answer is **b**.

5. What is this picture all about?
   a. a band concert
   b. shoppers in a city
   c. a parade on a city street

Check your answer. Add up all the details in the picture to find the main idea. The right answer is **c**.

LESSON 1

What is this story about? Add up the details to find the main idea. Finding the main idea will help you understand the story.

Snake Crossing

You have probably heard of a deer crossing. It's a road that deer go across. In one national forest, there is a snake crossing. Twice a year, the only traffic on the road is snakes. The road is closed so that the snakes can get across.

The road is closed in the spring, from April 14 to April 25. It is closed again in the fall, from September 24 to October 15. In April, the snakes travel about 500 feet from their winter homes. They head for the swamps and stay there in warm weather. In October, the snakes cover the same distance to go back.

The snakes would have trouble crossing a road filled with cars. So the road is closed to traffic when the snakes are crossing.

No one knows how many snakes cross the road each time. Many of the snakes are poisonous and dangerous. That is why no one gets close enough to count them.

Choose the best answer for each question.

1. What is the main idea of this story?
   a. Snakes can be dangerous.
   b. Snakes live in swamps in warm weather.
   c. Snakes cross a road several times a year.

Check your answer. Only one answer tells what the story is mostly about. The other two answers give details in the story. The right answer is **c**.

2. Another good title for this story is ___.
   a. "Snake Traffic"
   b. "Snakes in the Spring"
   c. "Too Many Cars"

Check your answer. A good title tells something about the main idea. The answer is **a**.

3. Where is the snake crossing?
   a. in a city
   b. in a forest
   c. in a parking lot

Check your answer. This question asks about a detail in the story. Find the right detail in the first paragraph. The answer is **b**.

4. The snakes head for the swamps in ___.
   a. September
   b. October
   c. April

Check your answer. Find a sentence about the swamps. When do the snakes go there? The answer is **c**.

5. No one gets close enough to count the snakes because ___.
   a. there are too many of them
   b. they are dangerous
   c. they move too fast

Check your answer. The last part of the story tells *why* no one counts the snakes. The answer is **b**.

LESSON 2

The title of this story helps to tell the main idea. Think about the title while you read the story.

Watch Out for Burglars

Is your home safe from burglars? Here are some tips on how to keep your home safe. These tips come from a burglar who has "gone straight."

One way to keep a burglar out is to make sure that someone is home. A burglar would rather try an empty house. You may be able to fool a burglar by keeping a light on when you are out. Another trick is to leave a radio on.

Suppose you will be away for one or more days. Here are some things to do. Keep a light on. Lock your doors and windows. Make sure that no newspapers are left at your door. Tell the post office to hold your mail. A pile of newspapers and a full mailbox tell a burglar, "Come in."

Be prepared in case a burglar does get in. Make it hard for the burglar to sell your property. Ask your police station how to mark your valuable things. Keep a list of the numbers you mark on your TV set, typewriter, and other items.

Choose the best answer for each question.

1. This story is mostly about ___.
   a. catching a burglar
   b. marking your TV set
   c. keeping burglars out of your home

2. Another title that tells the main idea is ___.
   a. "A Safer Home"
   b. "A Light in the Window"
   c. "A Burglar's Life"

3. The tips in the story come from a person who used to be ___.
   a. a policeman
   b. a burglar
   c. a carpenter

4. Leave a radio on so a burglar will think that ___.
   a. someone likes music
   b. a window is open
   c. someone is home

5. Why should you mark a number on your TV set?
   a. It will be harder to carry.
   b. It will be harder to sell.
   c. It will be more valuable.

Check your answers.

Question 1: Only one answer tells what the story is *mostly* about. The answer is **c**.

Question 2: You have to know the main idea to choose the right title. The answer is **a**.

Question 3: This question asks about a detail in the story. Look back at the first paragraph to find the right detail. The answer is **b**.

Question 4: Find a sentence about having a radio on. Look for details in the same paragraph. The answer is **c**.

Question 5: The last part of the story tells why you should mark valuable items. The answer is **b**.

LESSON 3

Practice finding the main idea and the details in the next stories.

The Search for Gold

The Barents Sea is near the Soviet Union. The water in this sea is icy cold. It is much too cold for swimming. Yet, in the fall of 1981, divers started swimming around in the Barents Sea. They were looking for gold.

There isn't usually any gold in the sea. This gold had been on a ship, however. During World War II, a ship from Great Britain was carrying the gold from the Soviet Union to the U.S. A German boat sank the ship. Since 1942, the gold and the ship have sat on the bottom of the sea.

The gold was valuable, but no one went after it. The water was so cold and deep that divers could not swim there. But a new kind of diving suit has changed all that. Now divers can stay warm in icy water. The search for the gold could begin.

What will happen to the gold when it is found? The diving company will get almost half. The Soviet Union and Great Britain will divide up the rest.

Choose the best answer for each question.

1. This story is mainly about ___.
   a. the gold in the Barents Sea
   b. a ship that sank in 1942
   c. a new kind of diving suit

2. Another good title for this story is ___.
   a. "The War Between Ships"
   b. "Diving Lessons"
   c. "Treasure in the Sea"

3. When did World War II take place?
   a. in the 1920's
   b. in the 1940's
   c. in 1981

4. What happened to the gold on the ship?
   a. It melted.
   b. It went down in the sea.
   c. It turned into ice.

5. Divers could not search for the gold because ___.
   a. the water was too cold
   b. there were no diving suits
   c. the gold had disappeared

6. Which two countries will get some of the gold?
   a. the Soviet Union and the United States
   b. Germany and Great Britain
   c. Great Britain and the Soviet Union

LESSON 4

A New Look for Hens

Someday hens may be wearing contact lenses. The hens won't be able to see better, but they will probably lay more eggs. This story tells why.

Hens do a lot of fighting. They peck at each other to show who's boss. One of the hens may start to bleed. The other hens will see the blood and will kill the hurt hen. A farmer can lose many hens this way and also many eggs.

A scientist from Virginia has found a way to stop the hens from killing each other. He has made a contact lens that fits over a hen's eye. This lens is not as clear as the kind that people wear. It is also colored light red. Everything the hen sees will look red, and a little fuzzy. Then the hens won't be so quick to notice that another hen is bleeding. The hens might spend less time pecking at each other and more time laying eggs.

A contact lens would stay in a hen's eye for about a year. That is how long a hen lays eggs.

Choose the best answer for each question.

1. What is the main idea of this story?
   a. Hens like to fight.
   b. Hens may wear contact lenses.
   c. Hens lay many eggs in a year.

2. What makes the hens kill a hurt hen?
   a. the sight of its blood
   b. the look in its eye
   c. the number of eggs it has

3. What color is a contact lens for a hen?
   a. the same color as a hen's eye
   b. light red
   c. no color at all

4. Because of the contact lenses, farmers may have ___.
   a. eggs that look red
   b. bigger eggs
   c. more eggs

5. Who got the idea for a contact lens for hens?
   a. a farmer
   b. a cook
   c. a scientist

6. A hen keeps on laying eggs for __.
   a. one week
   b. about a year
   c. many years

A NEW LOOK FOR HENS

LESSON 5

The Right Spot

Suppose you want to open a new restaurant. How would you find the right spot to build the restaurant? How would you make sure that people would go there?

Those questions are important to people who open a new restaurant. They follow certain rules when they build the restaurant. Here are some rules from a company that owns a chain of steak restaurants.

First, choose a town or city that is growing. New people moving in will bring new business to a restaurant.

Build the restaurant on a street that people can get to easily. The street should have plenty of traffic, but the traffic shouldn't go by too fast. About 35 miles per hour is just right. At that speed, drivers will have no trouble turning off the road when they see the restaurant.

Plan a new restaurant *near* a shopping center, but not *in* it. A lot of stores together may hide a restaurant.

Finally, open your new restaurant near other eating places. People at other places will notice yours, too. Keep your restaurant away from places just like yours, however. Two steak restaurants side by side will have to share the business.

Choose the best answer for each question.

1. This story is mostly about ___.
   a. how to build a restaurant
   b. how to choose a place for a restaurant
   c. how to choose food for a restaurant

2. Another good title for this story is ___.
   a. "The Right Price"
   b. "New Restaurants in Town"
   c. "Where to Put a New Restaurant"

3. The speed limit for a street with a restaurant should be ___.
   a. 35 miles per hour or less
   b. 35 to 50 miles per hour
   c. 60 miles per hour

4. A restaurant in a shopping center may be ___.
   a. too crowded
   b. hard to find
   c. too noisy

5. The story says that a steak restaurant should not be ___.
   a. in a big town
   b. near a pizza place
   c. near other steak places

6. The rules in the story come from ___.
   a. people who own restaurants
   b. new people in cities
   c. drivers of fast cars

When Hiccups Happen

A hiccup gets its name from the sound it makes. A muscle in the chest tightens up. Air is pulled into the lungs. The air causes the vocal cords to move. That movement makes a loud "hic" sound.

We can't do much to keep hiccups from starting. Hiccups just happen, like breathing. Hiccups often start during a meal, or just after a meal. Worrying or being excited may cause hiccups.

Long ago, people blamed the hiccups on an evil spirit. No one knew the real cause, but there were hundreds of ideas for stopping the hiccups. Here are two examples. You could drink nine swallows of water without breathing. Or you could press a spot on the bottom of the neck.

Those two ideas still seem to work. Another idea is to breathe into a paper bag. Some people say they can be scared out of their hiccups, but being scared may be worse than having hiccups.

Hiccups usually go away, no matter what we do. A man from Iowa was not so lucky, however. He got the hiccups in 1922 and they lasted for more than 50 years.

Choose the best answer for each question.

1. Another good title for this story is __.
   a. "Hiccups and Evil Spirits"
   b. "Causes and Cures for Hiccups"
   c. "Scared Out of Hiccups"

2. The story says that one cause of hiccups may be __.
   a. laughing
   b. breathing
   c. worrying

3. Long ago, people didn't know __.
   a. why hiccups start
   b. how hiccups sound
   c. how to stop hiccups

4. One idea for stopping hiccups is to __.
   a. breathe into water
   b. eat more quickly
   c. breathe into a paper bag

5. The sound of a hiccup comes when ___.
　　a. the evil spirits fly
　　b. the vocal cords move
　　c. a paper bag breaks

6. It is a fact that hiccups don't usually ___.
　　a. start suddenly
　　b. start during a meal
　　c. last for 50 years

Spinning Wheels

Two young men went across the country on wheels. They didn't drive cars. They didn't ride bicycles. Instead, they went in wheelchairs.

The men are Phil Carpenter and George Murray. Both were hurt in accidents when they were younger. They can't walk and have to get around in wheelchairs. They wanted to show that people in wheelchairs could still do almost anything. Their dream was to push their wheelchairs across the U.S., a distance of 3,400 miles. "Our friends said we were crazy," said Phil and George.

They started off in Los Angeles in April, 1981. A friend drove a van behind them. They did all their traveling at night. There was less traffic at night, and it wasn't too hot.

One of the hardest parts of the trip was going over the Rocky Mountains. Phil and George got blisters on their hands from pushing their wheelchairs up the mountain roads. Going down was hard, too. Parachutes were tied to the wheelchairs to slow their speed.

New York City was the last stop for Phil and George. They got there in August, four months after starting out. They said, "Our friends still think we're crazy, but now they look at us in a different way."

Choose the best answer for each question.

1. What is the main idea of this story?
   a. Two men were hurt in accidents.
   b. Two men went 3,400 miles across the U.S.
   c. Two men went across the U.S. in wheelchairs.

2. Phil and George wanted to show that __.
   a. people in wheelchairs could walk
   b. people in wheelchairs could do hard things
   c. people in wheelchairs could laugh

3. The two men pushed their wheelchairs from __.
   a. Los Angeles to New York
   b. New York to Los Angeles
   c. Los Angeles to Chicago

4. Who traveled with Phil and George?
   a. a mountain climber
   b. a friend in a van
   c. a sky diver

5. Why did the men travel at night?
   a. They couldn't sleep.
   b. It was quieter.
   c. There were fewer cars.

6. What kept the wheelchairs from going downhill too fast?
   a. new wheels
   b. mountain roads
   c. parachutes

Trouble in Texas

People in Texas are worrying about fire ants. Fire ants are not like other kinds of ants. They are much more dangerous. Fire ants may even cause death.

Fire ants usually live in the ground, but rain drives them out. There were heavy rains in Texas in the fall of 1981. The fire ants tried to escape from the soggy ground. They built their nests above the ground. That's when the trouble began. The nests were a foot high. People began to bump into the nests. The fire ants got angry. They wanted to protect the food inside their nests. So, sometimes they would sting. Scientists in Texas said that a few people may have died from the sting of fire ants.

It is very hard to get rid of fire ants. The ants came to the United States from South America in the 1930's. They have been spreading every year, from state to state. They reached Texas in 1956 and now cover nearly half the state. The ants spread by riding on almost anything that moves. They ride on the wind. They even ride on pickup trucks.

Choose the best answer for each question.

1. What is the main idea of this story?
   a. Fire ants are hurting people in Texas.
   b. Texas has a lot of rain.
   c. Fire ants ride on the wind.

2. Another good title for this story is __.
   a. "Nests of Fire Ants"
   b. "Where Fire Ants Come From"
   c. "Attack of the Fire Ants"

3. In 1981 the nests of fire ants got in the way because __.
   a. they fell over easily
   b. they stuck up high
   c. they blocked the streets

4. When fire ants get angry, what do they do?
   a. They sting.
   b. They ride on trucks.
   c. They bump into nests.

5. How do fire ants get around a state?
   a. They build high nests.
   b. They move in wet ground.
   c. They ride on the wind.

6. When did the first fire ants reach Texas?
   a. in the 1930's
   b. in 1956
   c. in 1981

TAKING TESTS

Practice finding a main idea in a reading selection. Follow the test tips on the next four pages. Put your answers on your answer sheet.

Test Tips: The title of a story helps to tell the main idea. Sometimes a story on a test has no title. Then you can usually find the main idea in the first few sentences.

The roller coaster is back. The king of the amusement park rides has had its ups and downs over the years. Now the roller coaster is more popular than ever.

Roller coasters first caught on in the 1920's. There were more than 1,500 of these rides in the world at that time. Starting in the 1940's, people lost interest in roller coasters. Now that feeling has changed. More than 100 roller coasters have gone up in the U.S. since 1970.

One of the newest roller coasters is the Thunderball Express in New York State. The tracks are made of steel and are 3,100 feet long and 120 feet high. Loops along the tracks turn riders completely upside down five times in a two-minute ride.

Speeds on new roller coasters can be as fast as 60 miles per hour. Early roller coasters reached a top speed of six miles per hour. They ran on wooden tracks.

---

1. What is the main idea of this story?
   a. Roller coasters are fast.
   b. Roller coasters are popular again.
   c. The U.S. has 100 roller coasters.
   d. A roller coaster has loops.

2. What is the best title for this selection?
   a. "King of the Rides"
   b. "New Roller Coasters"
   c. "Downhill Racer"
   d. "Roller Coasters of the Past"

3. Early roller coaster tracks were made of ___.
   a. iron   c. steel
   b. rubber   d. wood

4. How are riders turned upside down?
   a. The tracks are smooth.
   b. The tracks are wide.
   c. The tracks are high.
   d. The tracks have loops.

5. How many miles per hour can a roller coaster go now?
   a. 6   c. 60
   b. 12   d. 120

Test Tips: A poem has a main idea, like a story. Read a poem quickly the first time. You'll find the main idea more easily.

The sea gull curves his wings,
The sea gull turns his eyes.
Get down into the water, fish!
(If you are wise.)

The sea gull slants his wings,
The sea gull turns his head.
Get down into the water, fish!
(Or you'll be dead.)

Elizabeth Coatsworth

1. What is the main idea of this poem?
   a. A sea gull turns his wings.
   b. A sea gull goes after a fish.
   c. A fish swims in the water.
   d. A fish sees a sea gull.

2. Which of these is the best title for this poem?
   a. "The Sea Gull's Fishing"
   b. "The Sea Shore"
   c. "How to Catch Fish"
   d. "How to Cook Fish"

3. A picture of the main idea of this poem would show __.
   a. birds flying south
   b. a fishing boat
   c. fish in a net
   d. a bird flying down to the water

4. The poet wants the fish to __.
   a. jump out of the water
   b. close its eyes
   c. watch out for the sea gull
   d. talk to the sea gull

5. The poet thinks the fish will be safe __.
   a. in a boat
   b. in the air
   c. on top of the water
   d. under the water

TAKING TESTS

Test Tips: Some words in a story may be used over and over again. These words can help you figure out the main idea.

The cost of food has been going up. Shoppers in many stores are finding a way to cut their food bills. They are buying food in plain boxes, cans, or bottles. There is no brand name on the label. Instead, the label says CORN FLAKES or PEAS or POTATO CHIPS.

Food with a brand name always costs more than food with no brand name. Compare these prices, for example. In one store, a popular brand of potato chips cost $2.29 a pound at the end of 1981. Potato chips with no brand name were only $1.29 a pound. A popular brand of spaghetti was 73¢ for a one-pound box. Spaghetti in a plain box was 47¢ a pound.

There are no ads for the no-brand foods. That saves money for a shopper. Shoppers don't have to pay for fancy packages in many colors, either. The no-brand packages have no pictures.

Food with a brand name may look and taste a little better than no-brand food. However, many people believe that is not as important as saving money.

---

1. What is the main idea of this selection?
   a. Potato chips cost $2.29 a pound.
   b. The cost of food is going up.
   c. Food with no brand name costs less.
   d. Stores sell many kinds of food.

2. What is true about no-brand foods?
   a. They have no boxes.
   b. There are no ads for them.
   c. There are no potato chips.
   d. There are no labels.

3. Which of these is not on a box of no-brand spaghetti?
   a. a price
   b. a picture
   c. the word *spaghetti*
   d. the weight of the food

4. No-brand foods help a shopper to __.
   a. read a label
   b. eat more peas
   c. save time
   d. save money

5. Which of these is the best title for this article?
   a. "No-Brand Foods"
   b. "A Way to Check Prices"
   c. "Save Money on Spaghetti"
   d. "Ads for No-Brand Foods"

Test Tips: Sometimes each paragraph in a story has a different main idea. Notice where each paragraph begins.

---

¹Anyone can learn to take good pictures. Here are some helpful ideas you can follow.

²First, take your time. Learn to look through the camera. Remember that a camera "sees" everything. Use your eye to choose only the things you want to see.

³Keep the background simple when you take someone's picture. Get in close to the people in your picture. Too many objects around can make your picture confusing.

⁴Take black and white pictures on cloudy days. The clouds make the light soft, and shapes stand out more clearly. The best time to take pictures in color is just before the sun sets, or just after the sun sets. The colors of the sunlight will bring beautiful colors to your pictures.

⁵Here's a final tip. If you are taking pictures of someone, ask that person to do something. Your picture will seem more natural.

---

1. This story is mainly about __.
   a. how to take good pictures
   b. how to get a camera
   c. pictures in color
   d. pictures in black and white

2. A good time to take color pictures is __.
   a. at night
   b. just before the sun sets
   c. at 12 o'clock
   d. at 3 o'clock

3. What is the main idea of paragraph 3?
   a. taking pictures of people
   b. looking through the camera
   c. when to take pictures
   d. taking black and white pictures

4. Clouds are important for black and white pictures because __.
   a. the clouds hide the camera
   b. the sky is darker
   c. shapes are clearer
   d. the air is cooler

5. Paragraph 5 is mostly about __.
   a. using your eyes
   b. buying a camera
   c. colors in a picture
   d. the person in a picture

The picture on page 50 shows a man and his daughter. Use the details in the picture to figure out what they are doing. The following questions ask about some of those details.

Choose the best answer for each question.

1. The man is helping his daughter to __.
   a. write letters
   b. write a story
   c. write numbers

Check your answer. Notice the numbers on the slate that the man is holding. The answer is **c**.

2. In what way is the man helping his daughter to write?
   a. He is writing for her.
   b. He is guiding her hand.
   c. He is reading to her.

Check your answer. While the girl is writing, the father's hand is on top of her hand. The right answer is **b**.

3. The little girl is probably counting numbers by using __.
   a. the beads at the top of the slate
   b. her fingers
   c. her father's fingers

Check your answer. You can tell that the beads at the top of the slate can be counted one by one. The answer is **a**.

4. Where is the writing lesson taking place?
   a. in a school
   b. on a farm
   c. in a park

Check your answer. The father and daughter are sitting on a park bench. The answer is **c**.

5. How does the father probably feel about this writing lesson?
   a. He thinks it is silly.
   b. He is enjoying it.
   c. He wants it to end.

Check your answer. The man is sitting very close to his daughter and smiling as she writes. The answer is **b**.

LESSON 1

The answer to a question is not always in the story. You can tell what seems to be true, however. You can use the details in the story to figure out an answer. Read the next story.

The Post Office Bites Back

A dog is often called "man's best friend." But many dogs are not a postman's best friend. Every year, about 8,000 postmen are bitten by dogs.

The U.S. Postal Service is trying to do something about this problem. In some cities, postmen carry a special umbrella. It can be opened quickly if a dog comes near. Some dogs run away when the umbrella pops open. Other dogs attack the umbrella but not the postman.

Many postmen protect themselves with a spray called "Halt." If a dog attacks, the spray stings its eyes for a little while. This gives the postman time to get away.

Postmen also have the right to skip houses with dangerous dogs. They can skip a whole block if a dog is loose.

Finally, the Post Office is taking some dog owners to court. When a postman is bitten, it costs about $300 for doctor bills and sick pay. Now the dog owners must pay this cost.

The Post Office does not like doing all this. It simply wants dogs to be kept away when the postman comes around.

Choose the best answer for each question.

1. Many postmen are worried about __.
   a. heavy mailbags
   b. dogs that bite
   c. lost umbrellas

Check your answer. The answer is not in the story. Use the details to help you figure out the right answer. The answer is **b**.

2. Dogs run from the umbrella because __.
   a. they think it will rain
   b. the umbrella stings their eyes
   c. the umbrella scares them

Check your answer. From your reading, you know that the umbrella pops open quickly. Choose the answer that makes sense. The answer is **c**.

3. A family with a dangerous dog may not __.
   a. get any mail
   b. buy dog food
   c. use an umbrella

Check your answer. The story says that postmen can skip houses with dangerous dogs. The answer is **a**.

4. The Post Office probably wants dogs to be __.
   a. locked up in court
   b. taken to a doctor
   c. kept inside

Check your answer. Notice the word *probably* in the question. That means you will have to figure out what is true. Use the facts in the last paragraph. The answer is **c**.

5. What is the main idea of this story?
   a. taking dog owners to court
   b. keeping postmen safe from dogs
   c. carrying an umbrella

Check your answer. What is the story about? Add up the details in the story to find the main idea. The right answer is **b**.

LESSON 2

Think about the facts in this story. Then decide what seems to be true about the woman in the story.

The Highest Rank

The U.S. was fighting World War II in the 1940's. Mary Clarke decided to join the Army as a private. She was a young woman from Rochester, New York. She wanted to do something to help win the war.

Mary planned to leave the Army after the war was over. The war ended in 1945, but she did not leave. She changed her mind because a male commander said something to her. He told Mary that she would probably never become an officer. "That did it," said Mary Clarke.

She stayed in the Army for 36 years. No woman has ever stayed that long. She showed the commander that he was wrong. Not only did she become an officer. She became a major general in 1978. Mary Clarke had the highest rank of any woman in the Army. She was the first woman to run a big Army training center.

Major General Clarke left the Army for good on October 31, 1981. On her last day, the Army gave her a medal and held a parade in her honor.

Choose the best answer for each question.

1. A woman in the Army does not usually __.
   a. talk to the men
   b. walk in a parade
   c. become a major general

2. The commander must have made Mary feel __.
   a. happy
   b. angry
   c. tired

3. The Army must have thought that Mary Clarke __.
   a. did a good job
   b. left too soon
   c. stayed too long

4. Which of these is the lowest rank in the Army?
   a. major
   b. private
   c. major general

5. This story is mostly about __.
   a. a woman who joined the Army
   b. a woman who lived in Rochester
   c. a woman who became a major general

Check your answers.

Question 1: The answer to the question is not in the story. Use the facts in the story to figure out the right answer. The answer is **c**.

Question 2: The commander told Mary that she would never become an officer. Find that sentence in the story. Then choose the answer that makes sense. The answer is **b**.

Question 3: Look back at the last two sentences of the story. Then choose the right answer. The answer is **a**.

Question 4: From reading the story, you know that Mary joined the Army as a private and later became a major general. The answer is **b**.

Question 5: Choose the answer that tells the main idea of the story. The right answer is **c**.

LESSON 3

Read the next selections. Use the details to figure out the answer to each question.

The Story of a Bridge

The George Washington Bridge opened in 1931. This bridge connects New York and New Jersey. Many people call it the most beautiful bridge in the world.

Before the bridge was built, people took a ferry boat across the water. The bridge helped the area to grow quickly. People in New Jersey drove to jobs in New York. Then factories opened in New Jersey. People from New York drove there to work. In 1932, five million cars crossed the bridge. By 1980, the number of cars was 82 million.

Nearly 260 people now work on the bridge. You might think their work is boring, but you would be wrong.

One time an airplane landed on the bridge. Another time a truck filled with watermelons turned over. Once a long truck nearly drove off the bridge. The driver was saved as he hung over the water.

In 1980, the whole bridge had to be closed for seven hours. A truck on the bridge was carrying a highly dangerous gas. Suddenly, it began to leak, and no one could stop it. Police cleared a six-block area. Traffic was backed up for 30 miles. Finally, the leak was stopped with a four-dollar plug.

Choose the best answer for each question.

1. This story is mostly about ___.
   a. how a bridge was built
   b. factories in New Jersey
   c. the George Washington Bridge

2. New York and New Jersey must be separated by ___.
   a. a highway
   b. a body of water
   c. a mountain trail

3. How long has the George Washington Bridge been open?
   a. for five years
   b. for 20 years
   c. for more than 50 years

4. The number of cars crossing the bridge has probably __.
   a. gone up each year
   b. gone down each year
   c. stayed the same each year

5. The bridge was closed for seven hours when __.
   a. a car ran out of gas
   b. gas leaked from a truck
   c. gas was found in a watermelon

6. Police closed the bridge because __.
   a. the gas could have blown up
   b. the cars were too noisy
   c. an airplane might have landed

LESSON 4

The Laughing Bird

Walter Lantz and his wife, Gracie, were on their honeymoon in California. They couldn't sleep because a woodpecker kept knocking on their roof. Instead of getting mad, Walter just knocked back. The woodpecker knocked back, too. That funny bird gave Walter and Gracie an idea.

Walter's job was drawing cartoons for the movies. He decided to use a woodpecker in one of his cartoons. The bird showed up in a cartoon for the first time in 1941. He was a wild-looking bird with a crazy laugh. Walter and Gracie had a name for him: Woody Woodpecker.

Woody was a hit right away, but there was one problem. Walter had to find someone who could do Woody's voice in the cartoons. The hardest part of Woody's voice was his laugh.

Many people tried out for the part. They put their voices on records. Walter listened to the records over and over again. Only one voice seemed just right for Woody. Whose voice was it?

It was the voice of Gracie Lantz, Walter's wife. She had slipped her record in with the others. Gracie got the job. Ever since then, Woody and Gracie have been laughing with one voice.

Walter Lantz celebrated his 80th birthday with Gracie Lantz and Woody.

Choose the best answer for each question.

1. What is the main idea of this story?
   a. how to draw a cartoon
   b. how a cartoon bird was born
   c. how to laugh like a bird

2. The idea for Woody Woodpecker started with __.
   a. a real bird
   b. a bird in a cartoon
   c. a record

3. What was Walter Lantz's job?
   a. caring for birds
   b. drawing cartoons
   c. selling records

4. How did Walter choose a voice for Woody?
   a. from a movie
   b. from the radio
   c. from a record

5. Gracie Lantz was better than anyone else at __.
   a. laughing like Woody
   b. climbing like Woody
   c. walking like Woody

6. The voice of a cartoon character must be __.
   a. a woman's voice
   b. a human voice
   c. an animal's voice

Be Like the Bird

Be like the bird, who
Halting in his flight
On limb too slight
Feels it give way beneath him,
Yet sings
Knowing he has wings.

Victor Hugo

Night

A wolf
I considered myself
but
the owls are hooting
and
the night I fear.

Osage Indian

Choose the best answer for each question.

1. In Poem 1, what happens when the bird stops on a limb?
   a. The limb turns brown.
   b. The limb starts to bend.
   c. The limb grows leaves.

2. Why does the bird sing?
   a. He knows he may fall.
   b. He knows he can fly away.
   c. He knows other birds.

3. The poet believes that __.
   a. people should whistle like birds
   b. people should fly like birds
   c. people should be unafraid like birds

4. In Poem 2, the poet used to think he was __.
   a. as brave as a wolf
   b. as brave as an owl
   c. as scared as a wolf

5. What sound does the owl make?
   a. a shout
   b. a hoot
   c. a whistle

6. What is the poet afraid of at the end?
   a. a wolf in the woods
   b. an owl in a tree
   c. sounds in the night

LESSON 6

How a Pilot Became a Hero

Lowell Ferguson is a hero in the tiny town of Buffalo, Wyoming. He became a hero by making a mistake. He landed his plane at the wrong airport.

Buffalo is a town of 4,700 people. There is a small airport there for small planes. Jet planes can't use this airport because the runway is too short. At least, that's what the people of Buffalo thought until the night of July 31, 1979.

Lowell Ferguson was the pilot of a jet with 100 people on it. The jet was on its way to Sheridan, Wyoming. Sheridan is 35 miles from Buffalo. It has a larger airport, made for jets. Just before the landing, a piece of equipment on Lowell's plane stopped working. Lowell couldn't tell how far he was from Sheridan. He spotted an airport and brought the plane down.

The pilot had to use all his skill to keep the plane from going off the end of the short runway. Suddenly, he knew he had landed at the wrong airport.

Lowell's mistake brought trouble from the airline he worked for. He wasn't allowed to fly planes for a while. But the people in Buffalo were glad he had landed there. The story about the wrong airport was in many newspapers. The town of Buffalo was famous.

Two years after his mistake, Lowell Ferguson came back to Buffalo for a celebration. This time, his plane landed at exactly the right place.

Choose the best answer for each question.

1. Lowell Ferguson wanted to land in __.
   a. Buffalo
   b. Sheridan
   c. New York

2. Why did Lowell land at the wrong airport?
   a. He wanted to play a game.
   b. He wanted to be a hero.
   c. He made a mistake.

3. Jet planes need __.
   a. three pilots
   b. a long runway
   c. a small airport

4. This story is mostly about __.
   a. landing at the wrong airport
   b. flying a plane safely
   c. talking to people in Buffalo

5. After Lowell landed in Buffalo, he __.
   a. went to jail
   b. worked for a newspaper
   c. couldn't fly planes

6. At the end of the story, Lowell was probably in __.
   a. a jet
   b. a small plane
   c. a plane from Sheridan

LESSON 7

The Dangers of Smoking

People who buy cigarettes find a special note on each pack. The note warns that smoking is dangerous. Many doctors are happy to see that note.

Warnings about smoking go back to the early days of the U.S. In 1798, doctors were saying that smoking was bad for people. By 1900, most states had laws against selling cigarettes to young people. Some states did not even let adults buy them.

Many people did not like the laws. These people said there was no proof that smoking was dangerous. Now there is proof. An important study in 1964 showed a link between smoking and lung cancer. About 100,000 Americans die each year of lung cancer. Many of these people are smokers.

Today, some laws about smoking have changed. No cigarette ads can be put on TV or radio. Some public places have rules against smoking.

Many older smokers find they cannot stop. But they still do not like to see young people start smoking. A recent study showed that fewer high school students are smoking now than a few years ago. These students say they realize the dangers of smoking. People who do not smoke can add as much as ten years to their lives.

There are several free posters and booklets about teenagers and smoking. To get copies of these, call the local office of the American Cancer Society, or write to this address: American Cancer Society, 777 Third Avenue, New York, NY 10017.

Choose the best answer for each question.

1. An important study on smoking came out in __.
   a. 1798
   b. 1900
   c. 1964

2. The study showed a link between __.
   a. young people and adults
   b. smoking and lung cancer
   c. TV and radio

3. What would probably happen if everyone stopped smoking?
   a. Fewer people would die of lung cancer.
   b. Fewer people would watch TV.
   c. Fewer people would go to high school.

4. High school students are probably smoking less because ___.
   a. they want to be doctors
   b. they have no money for cigarettes
   c. they want to be healthy

5. What is the main idea of this article?
   a. Cigarette packs have a note.
   b. Smoking can be dangerous.
   c. No one can smoke in public.

6. The American Cancer Society will send ___.
   a. information about smoking
   b. free cigarettes
   c. medicine for sick people

Too Many Birthdays?

Most young people like to have birthday parties. But many older people do not like to think about their birthdays. Every birthday reminds them that they are coming closer to old age.

Why does old age bother people? Many people have worked nearly all their lives. You might think they would now want to stop and rest. Many older people do *not* want that. They don't want to stop working just because they are old. Companies often make workers leave their jobs at age 65. This rule makes many active workers angry.

People are afraid of old age for other reasons, too. Old people often get robbed, especially in cities. They feel that the streets are not safe for them.

People who can't care for themselves may have to live in nursing homes. Sometimes the care in these homes is poor. Patients live out their days feeling sad and lonely.

Old age doesn't have to be spent this way, however. Thousands of old people stay active by joining groups that help others. They help students and give advice to teenagers. They write letters and feed the sick in hospitals.

One active group is the Gray Panthers. Its leader is Maggie Kuhn, a woman in her 70's. The 30,000 members around the country hold weekly meetings and activities. They fight for laws to protect old people in nursing homes. Maggie Kuhn and the Gray Panthers know one thing for sure. Staying active helps people to live longer and happier lives.

Choose the best answer for each question.

1. People often stop working at age 65 because ___.
   a. they are forced to
   b. they have too much money
   c. they want to sleep

2. Many people probably want to work after age 65 because ___.
   a. they like to rest after work
   b. they have a birthday
   c. they still feel useful

3. Many old people stay active by ___.
   a. joining groups
   b. owning nursing homes
   c. having birthdays

4. Companies may think that workers over 65 __.
   a. know too much
   b. no longer work well
   c. go too fast

5. The Gray Panthers probably think that people should __.
   a. stop working before 60
   b. work as long as they can
   c. sleep on the job

6. This story is mostly about __.
   a. Maggie Kuhn
   b. hospitals
   c. old age

Maggie Kuhn (center) and other members of the Gray Panthers speak about their work. They are standing in front of the White House.

Birdfoot's Grampa

The Old Man
must have stopped our car
two dozen times to climb out
and gather into his hands
the small toads blinded
by our lights and leaping
like live drops of rain.

The rain was falling,
a mist around his white hair,
and I kept saying,
"You can't save them all,
accept it, get in,
we've got places to go."

But, leathery hands full
of wet brown life,
knee deep in the summer
roadside grass,
he just smiled and said,
"They have places to go, too."

Joseph Bruchac

Choose the best answer for each question.

1. Why did the old man get out of the car?
   a. to save the toads from being hit
   b. to see the road better at night
   c. to watch the toads in the grass

2. The toads must have been hard to catch because they were ___.
   a. small and sleepy
   b. brown and leathery
   c. wet and leaping around

3. What did the poet want the old man to do?
   a. chase the toads
   b. lie in the grass
   c. get back in the car

4. Where did the old man put the toads?
   a. in the car
   b. in the grass
   c. in his pocket

5. The old man seemed to be ___.
   a. angry
   b. in a hurry
   c. in no hurry

6. At what time of year does the poem take place?
   a. spring
   b. summer
   c. fall

The Story of Famous Amos

What do cookies and reading have to do with each other? Not much, you might think. But Wally Amos knows that cookies and reading go hand in hand.

Wally's aunt taught him to bake chocolate chip cookies when he was 12. Wally continued to bake them for many years. His friends loved the cookies. Many of his friends said that Wally should start his own cookie company. At first, Wally laughed at the idea. But he finally opened a cookie store in Los Angeles in 1975.

Soon "Famous Amos" cookies were the talk of the town. The small store grew quickly into a big business. Now the company makes 7,000 pounds of cookies a day. They are sent to stores across the country.

Cookies are important to Wally Amos. But cookies are only half of the Wally Amos story. In 1977, Amos was asked to give away cookies as prizes in a library program in California. Children got free bags of cookies if they read four books and wrote about them. Hundreds of children took part. Many children who couldn't read well became better readers.

Then Amos learned that children are not the only people with reading problems. More than 20 million adults in the U.S. can't read. Many of them have a hard time at work. Amos felt something had to be done. He became a leader in a group that teaches adults to read.

Now he visits different towns and cities. He talks about the reading program. He looks for people to teach reading to adults. Why does he do this work? He tells others: "I never would have gotten anywhere without knowing how to read."

Choose the best answer for each question.

1. When did Wally Amos go into the cookie business?
   a. when he was 12
   b. in 1975
   c. in 1977

2. Wally's business probably grew quickly because ___.
   a. he helped people to read
   b. he liked to bake
   c. people liked the cookies

70

3. Famous Amos cookies are sold ___.
   a. only in Los Angeles
   b. only in libraries
   c. in stores around the country

4. Cookies were probably used in a library program to ___.
   a. get more children to take part
   b. give children more time to eat
   c. help children read about cookies

5. Wally visits towns and cities to ___.
   a. read to children
   b. bake more cookies
   c. help more adults to read

6. This story is mainly about ___.
   a. running a library
   b. the work Wally Amos does
   c. making chocolate chip cookies

Coming Back to Life

[1]Hardly anyone in Washington State will ever forget this date: May 18, 1980. On that day, the volcano Mount St. Helens blew up. The top of the mountain exploded in a cloud of ash. Hot mud poured out and went roaring into the valley below.

[2]Mount St. Helens is near towns and farms. Many people lost their homes when the volcano blew up. Some people lost their lives. The blast killed millions of birds and animals. Thousands of trees blew down. The hot mud poured into rivers and killed the fish. Farmers' crops were lost.

[3]At first, people thought the land around the volcano would be dead for a thousand years. But signs of life began to show less than a year later. There are fish in the river again and animals on the mountain. Flowers are growing again. Farmers have raised new crops.

[4]People living near the volcano are still cleaning up. They are wiping up the mud and clearing the wood. They are also building new homes. Even with all this work, the land may not completely return to normal for 200 years.

[5]Scientists are studying Mount St. Helens and the land around it. Until that day in May, the volcano had been silent for 100 years. Now the scientists are trying to find out why it suddenly blew up. They also want to find ways of telling when a volcano is ready to blow up. Then people living near a volcano could be prepared.

Choose the best answer for each question.

1. What is the main idea of paragraph 1?
   a. Mount St. Helens blew up.
   b. Many fish were killed.
   c. Mud poured from the volcano.

2. People near the volcano are still cleaning up because ___.
   a. the people are slow workers
   b. the volcano caused so much harm
   c. another volcano blew up

3. What is the main idea of paragraph 3?
  a. Flowers are growing.
  b. People are cleaning up.
  c. The land shows new signs of life.

4. Mount St. Helens must have blown up in about what year?
  a. 1880
  b. 1900
  c. 1920

5. People want to know ___.
  a. how to save mud from a volcano
  b. how to stop a volcano from blowing up
  c. when a volcano will blow up

6. The article does not tell ___.
  a. when the volcano blew up
  b. what happened to fish
  c. why the volcano blew up

The Man Who Climbed a Building

George Willig loves to climb. He has climbed mountains for many years. In 1977, Willig decided to climb the second tallest building in the world—the World Trade Center in New York City. It is 110 floors high.

Willig planned his climb carefully. He made a special steel claw to fit on the outside of the building. He found strong rope to wrap around his body. Willig tested the equipment on the building five times late at night. Only his close friends knew about his plan.

Willig began his climb at 6:30 a.m. on May 26. Soon a crowd of people gathered on the street. They watched the 27-year-old man make his way up slowly. Willig was 20 feet high before police found out what he was doing. They ordered him to come down, but he refused.

The crowd got bigger as Willig climbed higher. Soon thousands of people were cheering. The police waited on the roof of the building.

At 10:05 a.m., Willig finally reached the top. Police asked for his autograph and then arrested him. At first, Willig was fined $250,000. But later the mayor of New York changed the fine to $1.10, or one penny for every floor of the building.

Why did George Willig climb the World Trade Center? Many people said he wanted to be famous. But Willig said that is not true. He said he did it for the joy and challenge of climbing.

Choose the best answer for each question.

1. How long did George Willig take to climb the building?
   a. one hour
   b. about 3½ hours
   c. about 5 hours

2. Why did Willig test his equipment five times?
   a. to make sure it was safe
   b. to show that he could count
   c. to see how heavy it was

3. Willig probably did not tell police about his plan because ___.
   a. he did not know how to find them
   b. he thought they would stop him
   c. he thought it would rain

4. What reason did Willig give for climbing the building?
   a. for money
   b. for autographs
   c. for the challenge

5. The police probably arrested Willig because he was ___.
   a. scaring people
   b. climbing too slowly
   c. breaking the law

6. What is the main idea of this story?
   a. climbing a mountain
   b. climbing a tall building
   c. building the World Trade Center

TAKING TESTS

Practice using details to figure out what a story means. Follow the test tips on the next three pages. Put your answers on your answer sheet.

Test Tips: Before you look at the four answers, decide on *your* answer. Then see if any answer matches yours. That answer could be right.

Should there be laws against billboards? Many roads in the U.S. are lined with billboards. These giant signs are used to advertise stores, restaurants, airplane trips, and other things. Many people think that billboards spoil the roads. Some people say that billboards are not safe because drivers watch the signs instead of the roads.

In 1965, the U.S. did pass a law about billboards. The law said that all big signs must be at least 660 feet from the edge of a U.S. highway. That law did not wipe out billboards, however. New billboards soon popped up. These were farther from the road than the old ones, but they were also bigger and brighter.

Some cities have taken action against billboards. Boulder, a city in Colorado, used to have a lot of billboards. The city passed a law to keep billboards out. Now there are no billboards on any of the roads around Boulder. In another part of Colorado, one woman wanted quicker action against billboards. So she took matters into her own hands. She cut down a 15-foot-high billboard with a chain saw.

---

1. A good title for this story would be __.
   a. "Changing Laws"
   b. "Signs of the Times"
   c. "Billboards in Boulder"
   d. "The Fight Against Billboards"

2. Billboards are most likely to be on roads that have __.
   a. two lanes
   b. heavy traffic
   c. many trees
   d. sharp turns

3. What would be the best way to keep billboards out of a city?
   a. chop them down
   b. pass a law
   c. build a fence
   d. close the roads

4. In 1965, a law was passed to move billboards __.
   a. closer to the highway
   b. 660 feet in the air
   c. farther from the highway
   d. closer to Colorado

Test Tips: Notice the steps in a passage that gives directions. Figure out how to follow the directions.

Crunchy Stuffed Apple

1 large red or yellow delicious apple
2 tablespoons peanut butter
2 tablespoons raisin-granola cereal
Lemon juice
Dash of ground cinnamon

Use a knife to cut a ½-inch slice from the top of the apple. Scoop out the inside of the apple with a spoon. Leave a shell ¼ inch thick. Sprinkle the cut edges and the inside with the lemon juice.

Take out the seeds. Chop the pieces of apple. Mix together the chopped apple, peanut butter, cereal, and cinnamon in a small bowl. Press the filling into the apple shell. Top with the apple slice.

Wrap the apple in plastic or a small sandwich bag. Keep in refrigerator until ready to eat. Makes 1.

1. The foods you need are in a list at the top so you can __.
   a. taste them
   b. chop them
   c. have them ready
   d. freeze them

2. What will happen if the shell of the apple is too thin?
   a. The apple will taste funny.
   b. The filling will come through.
   c. The apple will change color.
   d. The apple will spoil.

3. The slice of apple from the top should be __.
   a. put back on the apple
   b. thrown away
   c. cut into pieces
   d. mixed with lemon juice

4. A *dash* of cinnamon probably means __.
   a. ½ cup
   b. two tablespoons
   c. a tiny amount
   d. a dish of cinnamon

5. You use the same amount of cereal as __.
   a. apple pieces
   b. lemon juice
   c. cinnamon
   d. peanut butter

TAKING TESTS

Test Tips: A question after a story may begin with "Why." The answer may not be in the story. Use the details to choose an answer.

Many newspapers in U.S. cities have had to close down. Most are afternoon papers. More than 300 afternoon papers have shut down since 1970. Even big cities like Chicago, Newark, and Washington have lost their afternoon papers.

Why are so many newspapers dying? One reason is that the cost of printing has gone up. The price of paper has gone up, too. Delivery trucks cost more to run now. Newspapers cannot charge readers enough money to cover these costs.

Newspapers count on ads from stores to help pay for the paper. Lately, many people have moved to small towns outside the cities. These towns often have papers of their own. The stores put some of their ads in the town papers. The city papers cannot get enough ads.

Television has also hurt afternoon papers. Many people buy a morning paper on their way to work. But after work, they are likely to watch the news on television. The TV news is often more up-to-date than the news in an afternoon paper.

---

1. Why are many newspapers in the news now?
   a. They have more news.
   b. They are buying more trucks.
   c. They are going out of business.
   d. They are moving to small towns.

2. This article leads you to believe that __.
   a. people will buy more afternoon papers
   b. more people will put more ads in city papers
   c. the cost of printing will go down
   d. more afternoon papers will close

3. Why would stores put ads in a town newspaper?
   a. to make the stores close
   b. to reach the readers in the town
   c. to give news about the city
   d. to use the delivery trucks

4. The story says that many people get late news from __.
   a. radio
   b. television
   c. stores
   d. books

UNIT II
VOCABULARY

PART 1 *Words and Meaning*

You often have to explain the meaning of a new word you see in your reading or on a vocabulary test. In Part 1, you are going to learn three different ways to help you understand and explain what a new word means. First, you will learn to match new words with words that have almost the same meaning. Next, you will learn to match words with opposite meanings. Finally, you will learn to match words that sound alike but have different meanings.

Look at the objects in the picture below. Which two objects are used to do almost the same thing? Which two objects are used to do opposite things? Which two objects have names that sound alike?

WORDS WITH THE SAME MEANING

One way to explain what a new word means is to name another word that has almost the same meaning. Knowing about words with the same meaning can help you read better.

Suppose you see a hard word in a sentence you are reading. If you can put another word that means almost the same in place of the hard word, you can understand what the sentence means.

Read the paragraph below about a famous invention. Two words in the paragraph are printed in dark type.

The first toothbrush was made in 1770 by a man who was locked up in an English prison. The man's name was William Addis. Addis wanted to find a way to earn a living once his prison term **concluded**. One day he was scrubbing his teeth with a rag, the way most people cleaned their teeth. Suddenly an idea popped into his head. He took a piece of bone and attached some brush bristles to it. The new brush worked well. When he was **released** from prison, Addis began making and selling his toothbrushes.

One of the words in dark type means almost the same as *set free*. Which word do you think means *set free*?

One of the words in dark type means almost the same as *ended*. Which word do you think means *ended*?

Read the paragraph again. This time read the word *ended* in place of **concluded**. Also read the words *set free* in place of **released**. Did using the easier words help you to understand the paragraph?

Do the activities on the next two pages. You will learn more about words that have almost the same meanings.

A. Look at the words in List 1 below. They were all used in the paragraph about toothbrushes. You will find a word or phrase with almost the same meaning in List 2. Can you match the words that have almost the same meaning? Put your answers on your paper.

LIST 1
1. prison
2. earn
3. term
4. scrubbing
5. attached

LIST 2
a. put on
b. time
c. jail
d. cleaning
e. make or gain

Check your answers. Reread the paragraph on page 81. Read the words in List 2 in place of the words in List 1. Does the paragraph still make sense to you? If it does, then your answers are right.

B. Read the next paragraph about another famous invention. Notice the words in dark type.

The first high-heeled shoes were worn by a man and not by a woman. The shoes were **designed** for King Louis XIV of France. The king was **embarrassed** that he was very short. He was so upset that he ordered his **cobbler** to make him a pair of shoes with very high heels. Other men and women soon began wearing high-heeled shoes. In time, men **abandoned** the high shoes, but women continued to wear shoes with higher and higher heels. In fact, some shoes got to be so high that women couldn't walk in them. They needed to **employ** servants to lean on as they moved around.

Now try to answer the following questions about the words in dark type in the paragraph about shoes.

1. Which word means almost the same as *gave up?*
2. Which word means almost the same as *upset?*
3. Which word means almost the same as *hire?*
4. Which word means almost the same as *made?*
5. Which word means almost the same as *shoemaker?*

Check your answers. Reread the paragraph. Put the words from the questions in place of the words in dark type. Does the paragraph still make sense to you? If it does, then your answers are right.

C. Here are the kinds of questions you sometimes see on vocabulary tests. Look at the word in dark type at the top of each item. Then pick the answer that means the same as the word in dark type. Put your answers on your paper.

1. **concluded** the story
   a. read
   b. wrote
   c. ended

2. **abandoned** the plan
   a. gave up
   b. thought up
   c. set free

3. felt **embarrassed**
   a. happy
   b. upset
   c. lonely

4. **employ** three men
   a. meet
   b. hire
   c. annoy

Check your answers. You should have picked **c** for 1, **a** for 2, **b** for 3, and **b** for 4. If you didn't get those answers, read pages 81 and 82 again.

LESSON 1

Here are the eight new words in this lesson. Next to each new word is a word or phrase that has almost the same meaning. Look for the new words in the story below. Use the words with the same meaning to help you understand the lesson words.

demonstrate—show
adventurous—daring
intended—planned
neglected—forgot

encountered—met with
achieved—did
maximum—top or most
collided—crashed

Being First in the Worst Way

Have you ever wanted to do something that no one else has ever done? Being first can be very exciting. Being first can also be very dangerous. The two true stories below will **demonstrate** some of the problems of being first.

In 1759, Joseph Merlin wanted to do something **adventurous** at a party. He decided to put wheels on a special pair of shoes and roll into a party. He **intended** to play his violin while he rolled in on the world's first roller skates. Merlin had one problem. He **neglected** to learn how to stop his skates. He came into the party and kept rolling until he **encountered** a mirror. He broke the mirror and his violin.

A French inventor named Nicholas Cugnot also had a hard time being first. In 1769, Cugnot **achieved** something wonderful. He created the first car that didn't need a horse to pull it. It was powered by steam. Cugnot's car reached a **maximum** speed of 2½ miles per hour. Cugnot also had trouble stopping, however. His automobile **collided** with a wall and knocked it over. This was the first car accident in history.

A. Here are the meanings of the new words in this lesson. Can you write the word that goes with each meaning? For help, reread the words or phrases beside the new words on page 84. Also look at the way the new words were used in the story.

1. planned to do something
2. met with something that was not expected
3. top or highest
4. exciting or daring
5. forgot to do or think about something
6. ran into or crashed
7. explain something by showing examples
8. did something very good

B. Look at the word in dark type in each item below. Decide which answer means almost the same as the word in dark type. Put your answers on your paper.

1. neglected to attend
  a. tried
  b. forgot
  c. planned

2. demonstrate the experiment
  a. show
  b. did
  c. try out

3. the **maximum** amount
  a. lowest
  b. highest
  c. correct

4. intended to study
  a. forgot
  b. tried
  c. planned

C. Write a sentence to answer each question below. Use the lesson word in dark type in your sentence.

1. What is the most **adventurous** thing you ever tried to do?
2. What usually happens to a car when it **collides** with a wall?
3. Where did you **encounter** someone you didn't expect to see?

Here are the eight new words in this lesson. Next to each word is a word or phrase that has almost the same meaning. Look for the new words in the story below. Use the words with the same meaning to help you understand the lesson words.

species—kind   **capture**—catch
consume—eat   **annoy**—bother
positive—good   **climate**—weather
negative—bad   **survive**—stay alive

Living Roach Traps

A new product is being sold to get rid of cockroaches. The product does not come in a box or can. It is alive. The new product is a **species** of lizard called a gecko.

Geckos eat roaches. One gecko can **consume** up to two dozen roaches every day. That is the **positive** side to owning geckos.

There is also a **negative** side to owning geckos. For one thing, geckos will bite people. They won't kill anyone, but their bite can hurt. For another thing, geckos are hard to **capture** once they are set loose in a house. They run behind curtains or under furniture. They run on walls or ceilings. They can **annoy** people in a house almost as much as roaches do.

Geckos are also used to a warm **climate**. They cannot **survive** in a cold home. So people who own geckos have to be careful when they open their windows and doors in the winter.

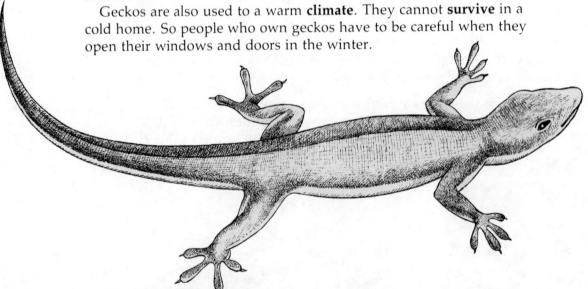

A. Here are the meanings of the new words in this lesson. Can you write the word that goes with each meaning? For help, reread the words or phrases beside the new words on page 86. Also, look at the way the new words were used in the story.

1. weather conditions of a place
2. good or helpful
3. bother or disturb
4. take or catch by force
5. bad or harmful
6. a single kind of plant or animal
7. continue to live
8. use up or eat

B. Look at the word in dark type in each item below. Decide which answer means almost the same as the word in dark type. Put your answers on your paper.

1. a **positive** sign
   a. large
   b. good
   c. bad

2. **consume** a meal
   a. fix
   b. prepare
   c. eat

3. **survive** the danger
   a. live through
   b. notice
   c. be afraid of

4. very mild **climate**
   a. colors
   b. feelings
   c. weather

C. Write a sentence to answer each question below. Use the lesson word in dark type in your sentence.

1. What is the name of another **species** of lizards besides geckos?
2. What is one **negative** thing that cockroaches do?
3. What is the best way to **capture** a cockroach?

LESSON 3

Here are the eight new words in this lesson. Next to each word is a word or phrase that has almost the same meaning. Look for the new words in the story below. Use the words with the same meanings to help you understand the lesson words.

flee—run away
employees—workers
pursued—chased
proceeded—went on

approximately—nearly
offender—criminal
swiftness—quickness
estimate—judge or guess

Racing Against Crime

A thief in Eugene, Oregon, found out the hard way that he couldn't run away from his punishment. The man walked into a store that sold running shoes. He put on a pair and then tried to **flee** from the store wearing them.

The thief didn't know that the **employees** in the store were both champion runners. The workers, Kevin Myers and Kelly Jensen, **pursued** the thief. The chase **proceeded** through streets and alleys. Finally, the employees caught the thief after they had all run **approximately** three-quarters of a mile.

Police arrived soon after and arrested the **offender**. He told police that he thought he had the **swiftness** to get away with the crime. However, he did not correctly **estimate** the employees' speed. He did not know that Myers was a top long-distance runner or that Jensen had tried out for the U.S. Olympic team.

A. Here are the meanings of the new words in this lesson. Can you write the word that goes with each meaning? For help, reread the words or phrases beside the new words at the top of this page. Also, look at the way the new words were used in the story.

1. run away from or escape
2. went on or continued forward
3. speed or quickness
4. make a judgment or guess
5. chased after
6. people hired to work for someone
7. nearly reaching an amount
8. someone who breaks the law

B. Read the beginning of each sentence below. Decide which answer is the best ending for the sentence. Put your answers on your paper.

1. An **offender** is someone who __.
   a. runs away
   b. breaks the law
   c. chases someone

2. When you **estimate** something, you __.
   a. run after it
   b. steal it
   c. make a guess

3. **Employees** are people who __.
   a. work
   b. annoy
   c. are fast

4. People who have **swiftness** are __.
   a. slow
   b. fast
   c. criminals

C. Write a sentence to answer each question below. Use the lesson word in dark type in your sentence.

1. Approximately how far can you run without stopping?
2. Would you **pursue** someone who stole something from you? Why?
3. How tall do you **estimate** your English teacher is?

Here are the eight new words in this lesson. Next to each word is a word or phrase that has almost the same meaning. Look for the new words in the story below. Use the words with the same meanings to help you understand the lesson words.

athlete—sports player
triumphed—won
participate—take part
stride—step

rotate—turn
transfer—shift or move
series—group
ambitions—goals

A Champion Racewalker

Tanya McIntosh can walk faster than many people can run. Tanya is a racewalker. She is only a teenager, but she is already a top **athlete**. She has **triumphed** in several national meets.

Racewalking is a sport in which more and more people are starting to **participate**. It looks easy, but it's not.

In racewalking, one foot must always be touching the ground. Walkers move by placing one foot directly in front of the other one in a long **stride**. They **rotate** their hips during the stride. Then they **transfer** their body weight from the heel to the toes and push off for the next step. At the same time, they pump their arms. Tanya pumps her arms in a way that looks like a **series** of boxing jabs.

Tanya started racewalking when she was 10. Since then she has set several future goals. Her **ambitions** are to walk a mile in less than eight minutes and to make the U.S. Olympic team.

A. Here are the meanings of the new words in this lesson. Can you write the word that goes with each meaning?

1. take part or join in
2. shift or move from one place to another
3. strong hopes or goals
4. gained a victory or won
5. turn something around
6. a group of things that go together
7. someone good at sports
8. a walking step

B. Read each incomplete sentence below. Choose the answer that best completes the sentence. Put your answers on your paper.

1. When you **rotate** your body, you __.
   a. fall
   b. turn
   c. stop

2. To **triumph** in a race is to __.
   a. lose
   b. finish
   c. win

3. A **series** of ideas is a __ of thoughts.
   a. dream
   b. group
   c. mistake

4. If you have **ambitions,** you have __.
   a. goals
   b. money
   c. friends

C. Write a sentence to answer each question below. Use the lesson word in dark type in your sentence.

1. Who are the top **athletes** in your school?
2. How many **strides** would you need to walk across the classroom?
3. What sports do you like to **participate** in?

LESSON 5

Here are the eight new words in this lesson. Next to each new word is a word or phrase that has almost the same meaning. Look for the new words in the story below. Use the words with the same meaning to help you understand the lesson words.

popular—well-liked
shudder—shake or tremble
anxious—worried or nervous
perilous—dangerous

heed—pay attention to
suspense—mystery
humorous—funny
tension—nervousness

The Master of Mysteries

Alfred Hitchcock may be the most famous movie director ever. His movies are so **popular** because they bring out strong feelings in people who see the movies. Viewers often scream, laugh, **shudder**, or even close their eyes during different scenes.

Hitchcock was an expert in making viewers and characters feel **anxious**. His characters often get caught in **perilous** situations that they don't understand. During these scenes, Hitchcock lets viewers know what the danger is. The audience wants to warn the characters to watch out, but the characters can't **heed** the warnings.

In most **suspense** movies, dangerous things happen in dark, scary places. In Hitchcock movies, bad things usually happen in light, "safe" places. For example, in the movie *The Birds*, a woman calmly sits in a park near a school. She doesn't know that birds are trying to take over her town. She sees one black bird sit on a jungle gym. The next time she looks, thousands of birds have gathered around her. Soon the birds attack her and the school children.

Another part of Hitchcock's style is to put something **humorous** into a scary scene. He knew that people often laugh when they are scared. The funny parts in the movies add to the **tension** that the audience feels while watching.

Some of Hitchcock's most famous movies are *The Birds, North by Northwest, Rear Window,* and *Shadow of a Doubt.*

A. Here are the meanings of the new words in this lesson. Can you write the word that goes with each meaning? For help, reread the words or phrases beside the new words on page 92. Also, look at the way the lesson words were used in the story.

1. a feeling of mystery or doubt
2. pay attention to what someone says
3. funny or amusing
4. shake or tremble because of fear
5. worried or nervous about something
6. a feeling of nervousness
7. well-liked by many people
8. likely to lead to danger

B. Look at each sentence below. Decide which answer is the best word to take the place of the word in dark type in the sentence. Put your answers on your paper.

1. As he watched the scary scene, the man began to **shake**.
   a. laugh
   b. shudder
   c. scream

2. The **nervous** woman looked for her lost child.
   a. anxious
   b. perilous
   c. humorous

3. The music added to the movie's **mystery**.
   a. popularity
   b. humor
   c. suspense

4. The speaker told a **funny** story at the beginning of his talk.
   a. popular
   b. humorous
   c. suspenseful

C. Write a sentence to answer each question below. Use the lesson word in dark type in your sentence.

1. Why do people laugh when they feel **tension**?
2. What new movie is the most **popular** with students in your school?
3. When were you once in a **perilous** situation?

WORDS WITH OPPOSITE MEANINGS

Some words mean just the opposite of each other. You can use an opposite to figure out the meaning of a new word. For example, the words *arrive* and *depart* are opposites. You probably know that *arrive* means *come to a place*. So you can figure out that *depart* must mean *leave*.

Sometimes you can change a word into its opposite by adding a letter group to the beginning of the word. Adding the letter group *un* or *dis* can change a word into its opposite. For example, *unhappy* means *not happy* and *disobey* means *not to obey*. Look for these word beginnings. They can help you figure out the meanings of new words.

Three words are in dark type in the following paragraph about a strange invention. Use opposites to help you tell the meanings of the new words.

Joseph Fallek **disliked** getting sprayed in the face when other people ate grapefruit. So he invented a grapefruit shield. The shield was a half-circle of thin metal with two needles at the bottom. The needles stuck into the sides of the fruit, and the shield went **atop** the fruit. The shield **prevented** juice from spraying other people at the table.

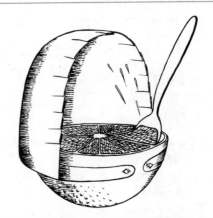

Here are the three new words and their opposites. Use the opposites to help you complete the sentences below the words. Put your answers on your paper.

disliked—liked or enjoyed
atop—below
prevented—allowed

1. If you did not enjoy something, you __ it.
2. If an object is not below something, it may be __.
3. If you are not allowed to do something, you are __ from doing it.

Do the activities on the next page. You will learn more about using opposites to explain the meanings of new words.

A. Read the following paragraph about another crazy invention. Notice the words in dark type.

In 1888 a new invention was created for people who had a **difficult** time getting up in the morning. It was called the EZ Wake Alarm Clock. The clock was hung above a person's bed. At a certain time, a piece of the clock would be **released** and drop onto the bed. One **harmful** thing about the clock was that the piece that was let go might hit the sleeper on the head. This was certainly a **disadvantage**. Most people felt very **uncomfortable** sleeping under the clock. Very few people bought EZ Wake Alarm Clocks.

Read each incomplete sentence below. Decide which word in dark type best completes the sentence. Put your answers on your paper.

1. *Helpful* is the opposite of ___.
2. *Comfortable* is the opposite of ___.
3. *Easy* is the opposite of ___.
4. *Advantage* is the opposite of ___.
5. *Held on to* is the opposite of ___.

Check your answers. Clues in the reading should help you figure out that the right answers are: 1. harmful, 2. uncomfortable, 3. difficult, 4. disadvantage, 5. released.

B. Read each vocabulary test item below. Choose the answer that means the opposite of the word in dark type. Make sure you choose an opposite. Don't choose a word with the same meaning. Put your answers on your paper.

1. released the information
  a. let go of
  b. held on to
  c. made up

2. an **unclear** idea
  a. strange
  b. smart
  c. clear

3. atop the building
  a. below
  b. beside
  c. above

4. feeling of **discomfort**
  a. sadness
  b. comfort
  c. pain

Check your answers. You should have picked **b** for 1, **c** for 2, **a** for 3, and **b** for 4.

Here are the eight new words in this lesson. Next to each new word is a word or phrase that has almost the same meaning. Look for the new words in the story below. Use the words with the same meaning to help you understand the lesson words.

assist—help
complex—hard to understand
permit—let or allow
distant—faraway

limited—cut short
illuminated—lit up
approaching—coming near
magnifies—makes larger

Tools That Help People See

In the past few years many new devices have been developed to **assist** people with sight problems. Some of the tools are fairly simple, but others are very **complex**.

Some simple tools are telescopic eyeglasses and glasses with mirrors built into them. Telescopic eyeglasses **permit** wearers to read books without holding them next to their eyes. They also help people see **distant** things more clearly. Glasses with mirrors help people whose field of sight is **limited**. These people can see things straight ahead but cannot see off to the side at the same time.

Some very complex tools have been created to help blind people walk around. One tool is a laser cane that sends out three beams of light. If the beams hit something, the cane makes sounds. The sounds warn a walker if something is in the way at head, waist, or foot level. One company has also invented traffic lights that make a different sound when each color light is **illuminated**. Another company has created talking street signs that tell what street a walker is **approaching**.

Even more complex machines have been created to help people read. One machine **magnifies** type to many times its printed size. Another has a computer that can see type on a page and say the words aloud.

A. Each word or phrase below means the opposite of one of the new words listed at the top of this page. Write the words and their opposites. For help, reread the words or phrases that have the same meaning.

1. leaving
2. nearby
3. simple
4. do not allow

5. dark or unlit
6. makes smaller or shrinks
7. made larger or increased
8. block or hinder

B. Choose the word or phrase that means the opposite of the word in dark type. Make sure you pick an opposite. Put your answers on your paper.

1. a **distant** place
   a. faraway
   b. disturb
   c. nearby

2. **approaching** a corner
   a. coming to
   b. leaving
   c. crossing

3. an **illuminated** lamp
   a. dark
   b. lit up
   c. broken

4. **magnifies** the letters
   a. makes larger
   b. makes smaller
   c. makes neater

C. Write a sentence to answer each question below. Use the lesson word in dark type in your sentence.

1. What are some tools people use to **assist** their hearing?
2. What **complex** tools do you know how to use?
3. How does a glass that **magnifies** permit people to see small things better?

Here are the eight new words in this lesson. Next to each new word is a word or phrase that has almost the same meaning. Look for the new words in the story below. Use the words with the same meaning to help you understand the lesson words.

accurate—correct
initial—first
unopened—closed
disbelief—lack of trust

unexpected—not hoped for
major—important
unpleasant—not nice
unnoticed—not seen

Perfect Predictions

In September, 1978, Mark Stone came to a TV station in Baltimore. He said he could make **accurate** predictions about what would happen in the 1978 World Series between the Dodgers and the Yankees. Two days before the **initial** game, Stone brought a metal box to the station. He said his predictions were locked in the box. The box would stay **unopened** until after the World Series.

After the final game, the box was opened on the air. An announcer read the predictions with **disbelief**. The announcer had thought Stone might make a few right guesses. What he saw was totally **unexpected**, however. Stone's paper listed the right score of every game. He had even written down some of the **major** events that had happened during the series.

Four months later Stone predicted the exact score and some important events of the Super Bowl. After his predictions were read on the air, however, someone made an **unpleasant** discovery. The person found that Stone's "locked and sealed box" had a false side. **Unnoticed**, Stone had been slipping his predictions into the box after the games were over. Mark Stone's career as a sports predictor was over.

A. Each word or phrase below means the opposite of one of the new words listed at the top of page 98. Write the new words and their opposites. For help, reread the words or phrases that have the same meaning. Also, look at the way the lesson words were used in the story.

1. expected or hoped for
2. open
3. belief or trust
4. seen or noticed
5. pleasant or nice
6. wrong
7. last
8. minor or not important

B. Read each incomplete sentence below. Decide which answer best completes the sentence. Put your answers on your paper.

1. Someone who feels **disbelief** does not __ something.
    a. agree with
    b. trust
    c. know

2. If an event is **unexpected**, it is not __.
    a. believed
    b. hoped for
    c. important

3. If an answer is **accurate**, it is not __.
    a. wrong
    b. right
    c. long

4. An **unpleasant** person is not __.
    a. correct
    b. sad
    c. nice

C. Write a sentence to answer each question below. Use the lesson word in dark type in your sentence.

1. Against what team does your school play its **initial** basketball game?
2. What was one **major** event that happened in school this week?
3. How can you make sure that a box stays **unopened**?

Here are the eight new words in this lesson. Next to each new word is a word or phrase that has almost the same meaning. Look for the new words in the story below. Use the words with the same meaning to help you understand the lesson words.

common—usual or normal
assistant—helper
conceal—hide
precisely—exactly

unsuspecting—trusting
unharmed—not hurt
disconnect—separate
unfastens—opens or unlocks

A Magic Secret

Sawing a woman in half is a **common** trick in many magic shows. Almost everyone has seen that trick performed. But how is it done? The secret is the table on which the magician puts the box containing the woman **assistant**. The table is built to **conceal** a second person inside.

When the first assistant climbs into the box, she sticks her head out one end. She also brings her knees up to her chest. At **precisely** the same time, the person hidden inside the table opens up a trick door below the box. The hidden person sticks her feet through the door and out the other end of the box. The **unsuspecting** audience believes that only one person is in the box.

The magician can now saw right through the middle of the box, and each assistant will be **unharmed**. The magician can even **disconnect** the two halves. When the box is put together again, the hidden assistant pulls her feet in and closes the trick door. The magician then **unfastens** the box. The first assistant steps out in one piece.

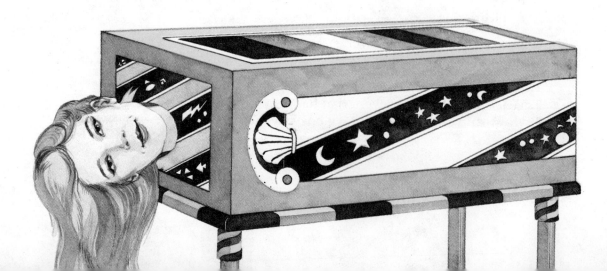

A. Each word or phrase below means the opposite of one of the new words listed on page 100. Write the new words and their opposites. For help, reread the words or phrases that have the same meaning. Also, look at the way the lesson words were used in the story.

1. boss
2. not exactly or wrongly
3. put together or connect
4. not trusting

5. hurt or harmed
6. locks
7. unusual
8. show or reveal

B. Look at each sentence below. Decide which answer is the opposite of the word in dark type in the sentence. Put your answers on your paper.

1. The woman tried to **conceal** her cat in her coat pocket.
  a. hide
  b. reveal
  c. put

2. The man was in a car accident, but he was **unharmed**.
  a. not hurt
  b. unlucky
  c. hurt

3. Sara was hired as an **assistant** in the factory.
  a. boss
  b. helper
  c. worker

4. The woman made sure she **precisely** followed the directions.
  a. quickly
  b. slowly
  c. wrongly

C. Write a sentence to answer each question below. Use the lesson word in dark type in your sentence.

1. What is a **common** act you see in a circus?
2. How quickly can you **unfasten** the lock to your school locker?
3. How can you **disconnect** a TV set from the electricity in your house?

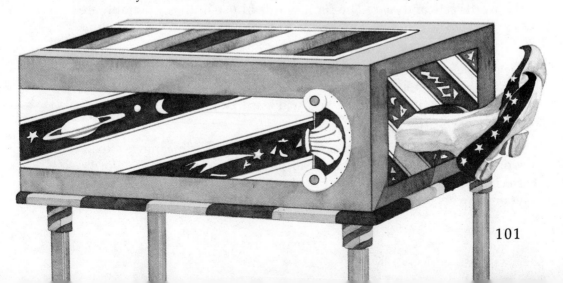

WORDS THAT SOUND ALIKE

Sometimes two words sound the same but are spelled in different ways. The two words also have different meanings. These *sound-alikes* can cause some problems in reading and writing. You have to be careful to make sure you are using the right word.

Look at the following paragraph about another strange invention. Two of the words in the paragraph are printed in dark type. The words are wrong. Each wrong word should have a sound-alike in its place. Do you know the right sound-alikes? Put your answers on your paper.

Many strange alarm clocks have been invented. One unusual clock had two ways of waking up a person. First, a bell would ring at the set **our**. Then, when the bell rang, a small metal arm would tip a cup filled with water. The water would run down a hose and **pore** onto the sleeping person. Very few water clocks were sold because most people didn't want to take a bath in bed.

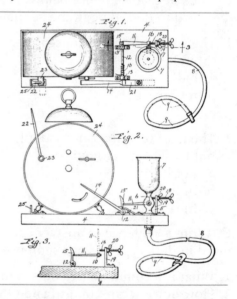

Check your answers. The words *our* and *hour* are sound-alikes. So are the words *pore* and *pour*. The right words to use in the paragraph are *hour* and *pour*.

Some other words in the paragraph also have sound-alikes. Look back at the paragraph. Can you find sound-alikes for the words *won* and *wood*? Write the sound-alikes on your paper.

Do the following activities. You will learn more about using the right sound-alikes.

A. Here are six more pairs of sound-alikes and their meanings. Read the words and the meanings. Then read the paragraph below the words. Decide which one of each pair of sound-alikes fits in the paragraph. Put your answers on your paper.

cause—make something happen
caws—the sounds crows make

flea—a small insect
flee—run away

shone—was shiny or glowed
shown—presented or demonstrated

scent—a smell
sent—had something carried away

weighs—measures heaviness
ways—how things are done

sight—the act of seeing
site—a place or location

In 1888, someone invented a new way to (cause, caws) mice and rats to (flea, flee) from a house. The invention was a picture of a cat cut out of cardboard. The cat was covered with special paint so that it (shone, shown) in the dark. An oil was added to the cat so that it smelled like peppermint. Rats don't like the (scent, sent) of peppermint. The invention was supposed to work in two (weighs, ways). The (sight, site) of the shiny cat would scare the rats. Then the scent of peppermint would make them run to someone else's house.

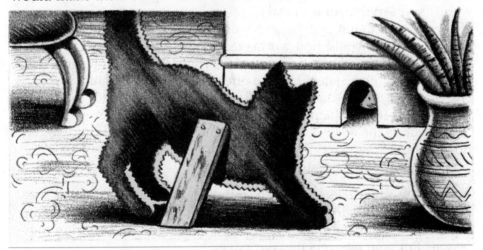

B. For each test item below, a definition is printed at the beginning. Choose the sentence in which the word in dark type has the same meaning as the definition given. Put your answers on your paper.

1. openings in the skin
   a. Sweat comes out of a person's **pores**.
   b. In hot weather sweat **pours** off a person.

2. was shiny
   a. The watch face **shone** in the dark.
   b. The salesperson has **shown** us several watches.

Here are the eight new words in this lesson and their meanings. Each new word has a sound-alike that sometimes confuses readers. Look for the new words in the story below. Notice how they are used.

lessen—make less or easier
groan—make a sad or painful
  sound
sense—good thinking
cheap—costing very little

praise—say something is good
grate—chop up
knead—mix by pushing together
dough—a mixture to be baked

Worms for Dinner

Ron Gaddie thinks he has a way to help **lessen** the problem of world hunger. His idea is that people should eat earthworms. The thought of eating worms makes many people **groan**, but Gaddie believes eating worms makes **sense**. Earthworms are high in protein that everyone needs. They are also **cheap** to raise, so most people could afford to buy worms and serve them for meals.

Gaddie says that if people gave worms a try, they would **praise** the new food. They would find worms tasty and healthful.

Gaddie knows a lot about worms because he owns the biggest worm farm in the United States. He also often eats worms. He adds baked, crisp earthworms to salads. He will even **grate** worms into small pieces. Then he will **knead** them into **dough** for oatmeal cookies.

Are worms the answer to world hunger? Ron Gaddie thinks so. What do you think?

A. Here are sound-alikes for each of the new words at the top of the page. Each sound-alike has a different spelling and meaning from a lesson word. Can you match each sound-alike with a word from the lesson? Put your answers on your paper.

1. lesson
2. cents
3. doe
4. prays

5. great
6. grown
7. cheep
8. need

B. Read each sentence below. Decide which sound-alike should go in the blank. Put your answers on your paper.

1. The students let out a __ when the teacher announced the homework.
   a. grown
   b. groan

2. You have to __ carrots before you make a carrot cake.
   a. great
   b. grate

3. The new notebook costs 89 __.
   a. cents
   b. sense

4. My parents gave me __ when I got an A on the test.
   a. prays
   b. praise

C. Write a sentence to answer each question below. Use the lesson word in dark type in your sentence.

1. What is one way to **lessen** the pain when your back hurts?
2. Which food is **cheap** to buy in school?
3. What things do you like to put in cookie **dough**?

LESSON 10

Here are the eight new words in this lesson and their meanings. Each word has a sound-alike that sometimes confuses readers. Look for the new words in the story below. Notice how the words are used.

aid—help
steal—take something illegally
wholly—totally or completely
vary—change or be different

herd—a group of animals
stationary—not moving
hale—healthy
lapse—pause

Knowing a Cow By Its Nose

You have probably heard of fingerprints, but do you know about noseprints? Noseprints are not for people. They are for cows. Farmers use noseprints to **aid** them in knowing if a cow belongs to them. Farmers also use noseprints to stop people who **steal** cattle.

A cow's nose has lines and circles on it just as a person's fingers do. No two cow noseprints are **wholly** alike. Noseprints **vary** from cow to cow. That is why a noseprint can help farmers know if a cow belongs to their **herd**.

It is not easy to take a noseprint from a cow. First, the farmer ties the cow to keep its head **stationary**. Then the farmer dries the cow's nose with a towel. (A **hale** cow has a wet nose just as a healthy dog does.) Next, the farmer puts an ink pad against the cow's nose and then presses a white card on the nose to take the print. The job has to be done fast. If there is a time **lapse**, the cow may lick the ink off.

Noseprinting is hard work. But it is cheaper and easier than putting a name tag on each cow. It is also less painful for cows than branding.

A. Here are sound-alikes for each of the new words at the top of the page. Each sound-alike has a different spelling and meaning from a lesson word. Can you match each sound-alike with a word from the lesson? Put your answers on your paper.

1. stationery
2. hail
3. aide
4. steel

5. very
6. heard
7. holy
8. laps

B. For each item below choose the sentence in which the word in dark type has the same meaning as the definition given. Put your answers on your paper.

1. pause
   a. There was a **lapse** in time between the first and second races.
   b. The runners each ran three **laps** around the track.

2. a kind of metal
   a. The new door was made of **steel**.
   b. Three men tried to **steal** the woman's ring.

3. listened to
   a. The **herd** of cows made a loud noise.
   b. We **heard** the cows as they made a loud noise.

4. not moving
   a. We put down the anchor so the boat would stay **stationary**.
   b. I bought some new **stationery** in the card store.

C. Write a sentence to answer each question below. Use the lesson word in dark type in your sentence.

1. How do fingerprints **aid** police?
2. Which two musical instruments sound almost **wholly** alike?
3. What is one way to tell if your pet is **hale**?

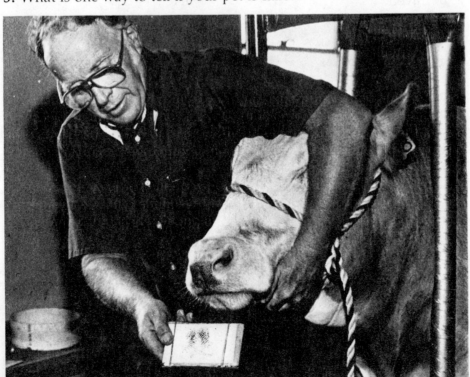

Choose the word or phrase that means the same, or almost the same, as each word in dark type. Put your answers on your answer sheet. The test words come from Lessons 1–3.

Test Tips: Carefully read the phrase with the word in dark type. Decide if you have ever heard the word or phrase before. Use your past knowledge to help you pick the answer that has almost the same meaning.

1. **encountered** a friend
   a. saw
   b. met with
   c. called
   d. remembered

2. **capture** a criminal
   a. catch
   b. jail
   c. rob
   d. stop

3. **estimate** the distance
   a. run
   b. travel
   c. guess
   d. time

4. group of **employees**
   a. workers
   b. animals
   c. numbers
   d. people

5. the **maximum** number
   a. smallest
   b. largest
   c. two
   d. mixed up

6. a **positive** action
   a. helpful
   b. daring
   c. possessive
   d. fast

7. **annoy** a neighbor
   a. move
   b. like
   c. hate
   d. bother

8. **pursued** by police
   a. caught
   b. stopped
   c. ran away
   d. chased

Choose the word or phrase that best completes each sentence. The key words in the sentences come from Lessons 4 and 5.

Test Tips: Read the sentence beginning carefully. Decide which word is the most important in the sentence. This is the key word. Look for the answer that means the same as the key word.

1. If you triumphed in a race, you __.
   a. lost
   b. almost won
   c. won
   d. fell

2. A popular song is __.
   a. long
   b. old
   c. well-liked
   d. not liked

3. People who are anxious are very __.
   a. nervous
   b. calm
   c. important
   d. happy

4. If you start to shudder, you are __.
   a. running
   b. moving
   c. talking
   d. shaking

5. A movie filled with suspense is __.
   a. funny
   b. mysterious
   c. happy
   d. boring

6. If you heed what someone says, you __.
   a. like the person
   b. know the person
   c. listen to the person
   d. forget the meaning

7. If you transfer from one job to another, you __.
   a. get fired
   b. change jobs
   c. make less money
   d. work hard

8. People who participate in a play __.
   a. watch it
   b. pay for it
   c. take part in it
   d. don't like it

TAKING TESTS

Choose the word or phrase that is most nearly the opposite of each word in dark type. Put your answers on your answer sheet. The test words come from Lessons 6–8.

Test Tips: Read all four answers carefully. Make sure you pick an opposite. Don't be tricked by a word with the same meaning or a word that looks like the test word.

1. **disconnect** two wires
   a. separate
   b. put together
   c. unroll
   d. touch

2. a **distant** location
   a. beautiful
   b. ugly
   c. nearby
   d. faraway

3. a **complex** idea
   a. simple
   b. smart
   c. stupid
   d. complete

4. an **accurate** guess
   a. close
   b. made up
   c. wrong
   d. estimated

5. **approaching** someone
   a. coming toward
   b. meeting
   c. going away from
   d. not seeing

6. **magnifies** the picture
   a. enlarges
   b. takes
   c. doesn't see
   d. shrinks

7. **conceal** the meaning
   a. show
   b. understand
   c. forget
   d. hide

8. **unfastens** the dress
   a. opens up
   b. closes up
   c. buys quickly
   d. sells quickly

Choose the sentence in which the word in dark type means the same as each definition given. The sound-alike words come from Lessons 9 and 10.

Test Tip: Try to put the definition in the place of the word in dark type in each sentence. Then see which sentence makes sense. Don't be tricked by a sound-alike or by a word with a different meaning.

1. ease or lighten
   a. Some people take aspirin to **lessen** pain.
   b. Studying helps you understand a **lesson**.
   c. Today's **lesson** was very easy.

2. say something is good
   a. My mother **prays** every Sunday.
   b. A cat often **preys** on mice.
   c. The teacher will **praise** my report.

3. pieces of falling ice
   a. The announcer said we might have **hail** tomorrow.
   b. The **hale** dog had a wet nose.
   c. The people will **hail** the new queen.

4. change or be different
   a. The weather will often **vary** from day to day.
   b. Tomorrow it will be **very** hot.
   c. Shana wears **very** different kinds of clothes.

5. not moving
   a. The **stationery** store has always been on that corner.
   b. Make sure a hurt person remains **stationary**.
   c. What kind of **stationery** did you buy?

6. mixture to be baked
   a. I didn't have enough **dough** to buy the book.
   b. My father prepared the bread **dough**.
   c. We saw a **doe** in the woods.

In Part 2, you are going to learn a good way to guess what a new word means. You will learn to look for meaning clues in the sentences and paragraphs that you read. Noticing how a word is used in your reading will help you guess the word's meaning. The other words in the paragraph will help you understand the new word.

Look at the picture below. The picture shows one meaning of the word **petrified**. Use the picture as a clue. What do you think **petrified** means?

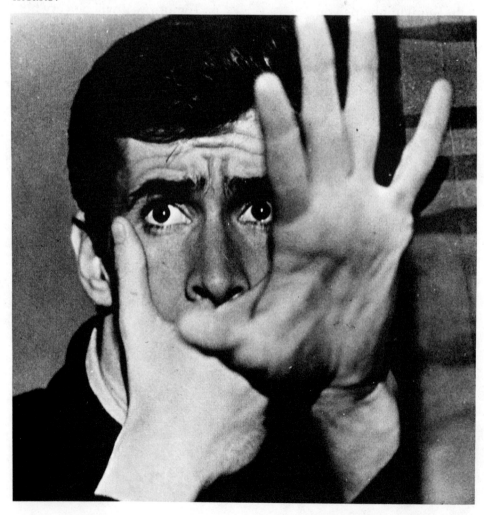

Suppose you are reading a story. You see a word you don't know. How can you figure out what the new word means? One good way is to look for clues in the words and sentences that come before and after the new word. The ideas that are around a new word are called its *context*. The meaning clues that you can spot near a new word are called *context clues*.

Practice using context clues with the following story about a popular food. One word is written in dark type. Can you figure out what the new word means? Look for context clues in the sentences before and after the new word.

A legend says that Hanson Crockett, a sea captain from Maine, first put a hole in a doughnut. Crockett was steering his boat and trying to eat a cake of fried dough at the same time. This wasn't easy because the sea was so **turbulent**. So Crockett pushed a hole in the doughnut. Then he could hang it on one of the handles of the wheel while he steered through the rough water.

Check your answer. Think about what happened. The captain was having a hard time steering. Was the sea probably calm or rough? The last sentence also mentions that the water was rough. All of these clues help you know that **turbulent** means *rough*.

You should look for different kinds of context clues when you read. You will learn to use five different kinds of clues in the following activities.

CLUE 1: DEFINITION CLUE

Sometimes you will find the meaning of a new word given right before or after the word. Look for a definition clue in the next paragraph to help you know what **indignant** means.

One day a guest at a restaurant in Saratoga Springs, New York, sent his fried potatoes back to the cook. He said the potatoes were too thick and soggy. The **indignant**, or angry, cook decided to get back at the guest. He cut the potatoes very thin and fried them until they were brown. The guest loved the new food, "potato chips."

Check your answer. The words *or angry* comes right after **indignant**. They tell you that **indignant** means *angry*.

CLUE 2: SERIES CLUE

Sometimes a new word will be part of a group of words that go together. You can figure out the meaning of the new word by looking at the other words in the series. Use a series clue in the next paragraph to help you know what **livestock** means.

American Indians have been growing popcorn for thousands of years. An Indian brought popcorn to the first Thanksgiving meal. Farmers also grow two other types of corn. Sweet corn is the kind we eat as a vegetable. Field corn is the kind farmers feed to cows, pigs, and other **livestock**.

Check your answer. The word *livestock* is in a series with *cows* and *pigs*. You can guess that **livestock** means *farm animals*.

CLUE 3: SAME MEANING CLUE

Sometimes you will find a word that has the same meaning as a new word. The same meaning clue may come in a different sentence in the reading. Look for a word that has the same meaning as **dealer** in the next food story.

Here is one story about the first ice cream cone. During the St. Louis World's Fair in 1904 an ice cream **dealer** ran out of paper dishes. Someone selling thin waffles nearby gave the ice cream seller a waffle. He wrapped it into a cone to hold the ice cream.

Check your answer. The ice cream **dealer** is also called an ice cream *seller* in the next sentence. You can guess that **dealer** means *seller*.

CLUE 4: OPPOSITE CLUE

Sometimes you can find a word in the reading that means the opposite of a new word. The opposite may be in another sentence. Look for an opposite below to help you guess what **solution** means.

Here is another story about the first ice cream cone. At the St. Louis fair, a man gave his girlfriend some flowers and an ice cream sandwich. She had a problem holding the flowers and eating the ice cream. The man had a **solution**. He wrapped one side of the sandwich around the flowers and the other side around the ice cream.

Check your answer. The word *problem* is used in the sentence before. It is an opposite of **solution**. You can guess that **solution** means *answer*.

CLUE 5: EXPERIENCE CLUE

Sometimes you can guess the meaning of a new word because the meaning makes sense to you. The meaning fits with things you know to be true. Use your experience to guess the meaning of **remedy** below.

Cola drinks were invented by a drugstore owner in Atlanta in 1866. He thought a drink made from coca leaves and cola nuts would be a **remedy** for headaches. He called the drink "Coca-Cola."

Check your answer. You know that drugstore owners try to help sick people cure themselves. You can guess that **remedy** means *cure*.

LESSON 1

Here are the eight new words in this lesson. Their meanings are not listed. Look for the words in the story at the bottom of this page. Try to find context clues to help you guess the meanings. You will find some hints to help you in the questions on the next page.

instance	**scraping**
commonplace	**temporarily**
secure	**substitute**
connect	**bogged**

A Car Emergency Kit

What can you do at a time when your car breaks down and you are not near a garage? You don't always need special tools in such an **instance**. You can use some **commonplace** things to get the car going again. You should keep such items as a scarf, a coat hanger, a pair of pantyhose, litter-box filler, a belt, and newspapers in your car trunk. These things will help you in an emergency.

A scarf can help repair a leaky hose. Wrap the scarf tightly around the dripping hose and **secure** it with a belt. The belt will keep the scarf in place until you can reach a garage. A coat hanger can help if the car tailpipe or muffler falls off. Wrap one end of the hanger around the pipe and **connect** the other end to the car's rear bumper. The hanger will keep the muffler from **scraping** along the ground. A dragging pipe could cause sparks. Pantyhose can take the place of a broken fan belt **temporarily**. It can **substitute** for the belt for a short time.

Litter-box filler and newspapers can help you get unstuck if you get **bogged** down in snow, ice, or mud. They will help the tires to move on the road.

A. Each question below gives you a hint about using context clues to understand the meaning of one of the new words in this lesson. Find each lesson word in the story on page 116. Then read the question about that word. Use the hint to help you pick the best meaning. Put your answers on your paper.

1. Find **instance** in the story. What word that means the same is used in the sentence before?
   a. time
   b. car
   c. garage

2. If *special* is the opposite of **commonplace**, you know that **commonplace** means ___.
   a. special
   b. different
   c. ordinary

3. Find **secure** in the story. What phrase that means the same is used in the next sentence?
   a. help repair
   b. keep in place
   c. can reach

4. Since you are putting the hanger on the car bumper, you can guess that **connect** means ___.
   a. break
   b. separate
   c. join

5. Find **scraping** in the story. What word that means the same is used in the next sentence?
   a. dragging
   b. cause
   c. connecting

6. Find **temporarily** in the story. What phrase that means the same is used in the next sentence?
   a. substitute for
   b. take the place of
   c. for a short time

7. Find **substitute** in the story. What phrase that means the same is used in the sentence before?
   a. for a short time
   b. take the place of
   c. can help

8. If *unstuck* is the opposite of **bogged**, you can guess that **bogged** means ___.
   a. stuck
   b. free
   c. stopped

B. Write a sentence to answer each question below. Use the lesson word in dark type in your sentence.

1. What are some **commonplace** things in your top dresser drawer?
2. What can you use to **substitute** for a pencil sharpener?
3. What is a good way to **connect** two pieces of wood?

117

LESSON 2

Here are the eight new words in this lesson. Their meanings are not listed. Look for the words in the story at the bottom of this page. Try to find context clues to help you guess the meanings. You will find some hints to help you in the questions on the next page.

departed	**physical**
reside	**tragedy**
autobiography	**surgery**
blend	**established**

A Japanese Hero in the U.S.

Toshiko d'Elia **departed** from Japan to come to the U.S. to live in 1951. She and her family **reside** in New Jersey now. Yet she is a hero to many women in Japan.

Toshiko is a versatile person. She does many things well. She teaches deaf children to speak. She is a runner who has set a world's record. She is also a writer. Toshiko has written an **autobiography**, the story of her life. The book is called *Running On*. The book is a bestseller in Japan and has even been made into a hit Japanese TV movie. Japanese women admire how Toshiko has been able to **blend** a job, a family, and sports.

In *Running On* Toshiko tells how she began running at age 44 to improve her **physical**, or body, strength. Toshiko also tells how running helped her six years later when a **tragedy** almost happened. The terrible event was the discovery that Toshiko had cancer. Doctors performed an operation on her. After her **surgery**, Toshiko was told to rest for a while. But a week later she felt strong enough to jog three miles. Four months later, she ran all 26 miles in the Boston Marathon. Then, four months after that, she **established** a world record for women over 50. She set her record by running a marathon in less than three hours.

A. Each question below gives you a hint about using context clues to understand the meaning of one of the new words in this lesson. Find each lesson word in the story on page 118. Then read the question about the word. Use the hint to help you pick the best meaning. Put your answers on your paper.

1. If *come to* is the opposite of *depart*, you can guess that **departed** means __.
   a. came to
   b. left
   c. stayed

2. Find **reside** in the story. What word that means almost the same is used in the sentence before?
   a. depart
   b. live
   c. is

3. The words right after **autobiography** help you know that it means __.
   a. story of your own life
   b. bestseller
   c. long book

4. If Toshiko does three things at the same time, you can guess that **blend** means __.
   a. try
   b. mix
   c. three

5. The words right after **physical** help you know that it means __.
   a. having to do with the body
   b. having to do with the mind
   c. having to do with running

6. Find **tragedy** in the story. What phrase in the next sentence has the same meaning?
   a. terrible event
   b. discovery
   c. an operation

7. Find **surgery** in the story. What word that means the same is used in the sentence before?
   a. performance
   b. rest
   c. operation

8. Find **established** in the story. What word in the next sentence has the same meaning?
   a. ran
   b. recorded
   c. set

B. Write a sentence to answer each question below. Use the lesson word in dark type in your answer.

1. What are some good ways to build up your **physical** strength?
2. Where do you **reside**?
3. What time did you **depart** from your house this morning?

LESSON 3

Here are the eight new words in this lesson. Their meanings are not listed. Look for the words in the story at the bottom of the page. Try to find context clues to help you guess the meanings. You will find some hints to help you in the questions on the next page.

gulped   cavern
vehicles   surface
collapsed   supports
cavity   drought

A Sinking Feeling

What would you think if the ground suddenly opened up and **gulped** down your house and backyard? You might think you were dreaming. But the ground really swallowed Mrs. Mae Owen's home in Winter Park, Florida. Several cars, a truck, and a few other **vehicles** fell into the ground. A parking lot, two streets, and a swimming pool also **collapsed** into the earth.

What was this terrible disaster that no one could stop? It was a *sinkhole*. A sinkhole is a **cavity** that forms far under the ground. The hole is made when chemicals in water and air mix to form acid. The acid burns holes into the layer of limestone rock which is under the ground in some parts of the world. During thousands of years the holes get bigger until they create a **cavern**, or underground cave. If the cavern gets big enough, it will swallow everything above it.

Why don't sinkholes happen all the time? The answer is water. Water inside the ground comes between the limestone and the **surface** of the earth. The water **supports** everything on the surface. If there is a long **drought**, a time of little rain, there may not be enough water to hold up the ground. That is what happened in Florida. Sinkholes have also occurred in other places around the word.

A. Each question below gives you a hint about using context clues to understand the meaning of one of the new words in this lesson. Find each lesson word in the story on page 120. Then read the question about that word. Use the hint to pick the best meaning. Put your answers on your paper.

1. What word that means the same as **gulped** is used two sentences later in the story?
   a. might think
   b. fell
   c. swallowed

2. Since you know that cars and trucks are things people ride in, you can guess **vehicles** means ___.
   a. holes
   b. things people ride in
   c. houses

3. Find **collapsed** in the story. What word that means the same is used in the sentence before?
   a. fell
   b. swallowed
   c. dreamed

4. Find **cavity** in the story. What word that means the same is used in the next sentence?
   a. ground
   b. chemical
   c. hole

5. The words right after **cavern** help you know that it means ___.
   a. limestone rock
   b. underground cave
   c. acid

6. If *inside* is the opposite of **surface**, you can guess that **surface** means ___.
   a. inside
   b. bottom
   c. outside

7. Find **supports** in the story. What phrase in the next sentence means almost the same thing?
   a. little rain
   b. may not be enough
   c. hold up

8. The words right after **drought** help you know that it means ___.
   a. enough water
   b. ground
   c. time of little rain

B. Write a sentence to answer each question below. Use the lesson word in dark type in your sentence.

1. What are some different **vehicles** you have seen?
2. What is the **surface** of the school made of?
3. What are some bad things that happen during a **drought**?

Here are the eight new words in this lesson. Their meanings are not listed. Look for the words in the story at the bottom of this page. Try to find context clues to help you guess the meanings. You will find some hints to help you in the questions on the next page.

fiction	**indestructible**
vessel	**sufficient**
destination	**submerge**
immense	**novel**

A Tale of Two Ships

This is a true story about two ships. One of the ships really existed. The other ship was made up by a writer of **fiction**.

The first **vessel** was called the *Titanic*. It set out on its first trip from a starting point in Southhampton, England, in April, 1912. Its **destination** was New York. The *Titanic* was the most **immense** boat ever built. In fact, the word *titanic* means huge. The *Titanic's* owners said it was **indestructible**, not able to be destroyed. But they were wrong. One night the ship hit an iceberg in the North Atlantic Ocean. It began to sink. The ship did not have **sufficient** lifeboats to save all the passengers. Because there were not enough lifeboats, many people died.

The second ship was described in a book by Morgan Robertson. Robertson called his ship the *Titan*. It was almost the same size as the *Titanic*. Its owners also said it could not sink. Yet the *Titan* did **submerge** on an April night after it hit an iceberg in the Atlantic. Many people died because there were not enough lifeboats.

You might think Robertson had copied the true story of the Titanic in his fiction book. But he had not. Robertson wrote his **novel** in 1898. That was 14 years before the *Titanic* sailed.

A. Each question below gives you a hint about using context clues to understand the meaning of one of the new words in this lesson. Find each lesson word in the story on page 122. Then read the question about that word. Use the hint to pick the best meaning. Put your answers on your paper.

1. If you know the story of the ship was made up, you can guess **fiction** means __.
   a. made-up writings
   b. true stories
   c. tales about ships

2. Find **vessel** in the story. What word that means the same is used in the sentence before?
   a. fiction
   b. story
   c. ship

3. If *starting point* is the opposite of **destination**, you can guess **destination** means __.
   a. home
   b. ending point
   c. first trip

4. Find **immense** in the story. What word that means the same is used in the next sentence?
   a. wrong
   b. fact
   c. huge

5. The words right after **indestructible** help you guess that it means __.
   a. destroyed
   b. not able to be destroyed
   c. wrong

6. What word that means the same as **sufficient** is used in the next sentence?
   a. enough
   b. lifeboats
   c. many

7. Find **submerge** in the story. What word that means the same is used in the sentence before?
   a. sink
   b. hit
   c. died

8. Find **novel** in the story. What phrase that means the same is used two sentences before?
   a. true story
   b. copy
   c. fiction book

B. Write a sentence to answer each question below. Use the lesson word in dark type in your sentence.

1. What is the title of a **novel** that you have read?
2. How many desks would be **sufficient** for your whole class?
3. What is one thing you own that is almost **indestructible**?

Here are the eight new words in this lesson. Their meanings are not listed. Look for the words in the story at the bottom of this page. Try to find context clues to help you guess the meanings. You will find some hints to help you in the questions on the next page.

confirm
transform
conversed
inquired

emerge
examination
inspected
vanished

The Great Gasoline Mystery

In 1917, Navy officer John Guthrie went to McKeesport, Pennsylvania, to **confirm** an amazing report. He wanted to check on a story that a mechanic named John Andrews could **transform**, or change, water into gasoline.

Guthrie **conversed** with Andrews' boss. The boss said that Andrews would sometimes put his special water into a customer's tank. It always worked. Guthrie then **inquired** whether Andrews added anything to the water. The boss answered that he didn't know. Andrews would take a bucket of well water and go into a shed. Minutes later he would **emerge** from the shed and fill the customer's tank from his water bucket. As a test, Andrews filled Guthrie's tank, and the officer drove all the way back to Washington.

A few days later Andrews came to a New York navy yard for another **examination**. He carried a small leather bag with him. He took some water and an empty can into the back seat of a Navy car. When he came out, the can was full. Several people **inspected** the liquid in the can. The liquid they studied looked and smelled like water. But it kept a boat motor running for a long time.

Andrews went home. A few days later the Navy tried to get in touch with him, but Andrews had **vanished**. No one ever saw him again or learned his secret.

A. Each question below gives you a hint about using context clues to understand the meaning of one of the new words in this lesson. Find each lesson word in the story on page 124. Then read the question about that word. Use the hint to pick the best meaning. Put your answers on your paper.

1. Find **confirm** in the story. What phrase in the next sentence means almost the same?
   a. wanted to
   b. check on
   c. change

2. The words right after **transform** help you know that it means ___.
   a. change
   b. check
   c. confirm

3. If you know that Guthrie and the boss spoke together, you can guess **conversed** means ___.
   a. met
   b. talked
   c. asked

4. If *answered* is the opposite of **inquired**, you can guess that **inquired** means ___.
   a. talked
   b. said
   c. asked

5. If *go into* is the opposite of **emerge**, you can guess that **emerge** means ___.
   a. come out
   b. stay inside
   c. go into

6. Find **examination** in the story. What word that means almost the same is used in the sentence before?
   a. tank
   b. drive
   c. test

7. Find **inspected** in the story. What word that means almost the same is used in the next sentence?
   a. looked
   b. studied
   c. smelled

8. If Andrews was never seen again, you can guess that **vanished** means ___.
   a. died
   b. disappeared
   c. gone home

B. Write a sentence to answer each question below. Use the lesson word in dark type in your sentence.

1. How can you **confirm** whether a battery works?
2. When did you **emerge** from your house this morning?
3. From whom can you **inquire** about a telephone number?

Choose the word or phrase that means the same, or almost the same, as each word in dark type. Put your answers on your answer sheet. The words in dark type come from Lessons 1–3.

Test Tips: Some answer choices are put in a test to trick you. Make sure you pick an answer that means the same as the word in dark type. Don't choose an answer that fits in the phrase but does not have the same meaning.

1. working **temporarily**
   a. slowly
   b. for a short time
   c. correctly
   d. quietly

2. **reside** on a boat
   a. sail
   b. travel
   c. decide
   d. live

3. **support** a weight
   a. hold up
   b. put down
   c. lose
   d. gain

4. live through a **tragedy**
   a. test
   b. adventure
   c. terrible event
   d. happy time

5. fall into a **cavern**
   a. car
   b. underground cave
   c. river
   d. doorway

6. **gulped** his food
   a. bought
   b. left
   c. cooked
   d. swallowed

7. wrote an **autobiography**
   a. story of one's own life
   b. book about animals
   c. newspaper story
   d. letter

8. **bogged** down in mud
   a. covered
   b. fell
   c. stuck
   d. stepped

Choose the word or phrase that means the same, or almost the same, as each word in dark type. The words in dark type come from Lessons 4 and 5.

Test Tips: Use context clues in the sentence to help you. Try to put your answer choice in place of the word in dark type. Decide if the sentence still has the same meaning.

---

1. The new cloth is supposed to be **indestructible** and long-lasting.
   a. expensive
   b. not able to be destroyed
   c. not expensive
   d. easy to sew

2. There were not **sufficient** books to go around in the class.
   a. enough
   b. too many
   c. new
   d. several

3. An **immense** cherry tree covers most of our front yard.
   a. beautiful
   b. tiny
   c. huge
   d. old

4. I called the station to **confirm** when the train would arrive.
   a. check on
   b. remember
   c. inspect
   d. test

5. The man **inquired** at the gas station for directions.
   a. stopped
   b. passed by
   c. filled up
   d. asked

6. The boat **submerged** in 50 feet of water.
   a. sailed
   b. sank
   c. stuck
   d. fell

7. Every spring caterpillars **transform** into butterflies.
   a. change
   b. get caught
   c. get eaten up
   d. forbid

8. The dentist **inspected** my teeth for cavities.
   a. holes
   b. studied
   c. cured
   d. filled

PART 3 *Words with Several Meanings*

In Part 3, you are going to learn some more new words. Each new word can have several different meanings. You will practice using context clues again. The clues will help you decide which meaning of a word fits in the story you are reading.

Look at the four pictures below. Each picture shows a different meaning of the same word. Can you guess what the secret word is? Do you know all four meanings of the word?

One word can have several different meanings. You need to look at the way the word is used in a sentence you are reading. That will help you know which meaning of the word fits in the sentence.

Look at these four sentences. The word *cast* is in each one. In each sentence *cast* has a different meaning.

1. The whole **cast** took their bows after the play.
2. The boy **cast** a stone through the store window.
3. Jeremy wore a **cast** that went from his knee to his foot.
4. The police made a **cast** of the robber's footprints.

Here are four different meanings of *cast*. Each meaning fits the way the word was used in one of the sentences you just read. Match the meanings with the sentences they fit. Put your answers on your paper.

a. a model or mold
b. a plaster covering for a broken bone
c. threw
d. a group of actors

Check your answers. Look at the way *cast* is used in each sentence. The correct matches are: 1. **d**, 2. **c**, 3. **b**, 4. **a**.

Think some more about words that have several meanings. How many different meanings can you think of for each of the following words?

club
fast
match
mind
mean
play
steer
wire

Do the activities on the next two pages. You will learn more about choosing the correct meaning of a word.

A. Read the following paragraph. Look at the way **direction** is used in the paragraph. Try to decide what **direction** means.

A football player named "Snooks" Dowd once ran 210 yards to score a touchdown. First he ran 100 yards in the wrong **direction**. Then he circled his goal for 10 yards. Finally, he ran another 100 yards to score.

Here are three different meanings of **direction**. Which one fits the way the word is used in the story?

1. an instruction about how to do something
2. a line in which something moves
3. the act of leading or running something

Check your answer. The meaning that fits the story is **2**.

B. One word is printed in dark type in each strange sports fact below. Decide which meaning below the fact fits the way the word in dark type is used. Put your answers on your paper.

1. Bert Campaneris and Cesar Tovar played in every **position** on a baseball field in one game.
    a. a job in a company
    b. a place something is in

2. Before 1930 many hockey referees **employed** small bells instead of whistles to call fouls.
    a. used
    b. hired to work

130

3. Some of the most **noted** hockey stars have worn number 9, while the most **noted** football runners have worn number 32.
 a. famous
 b. wrote down

4. Paul Anderson **performed** the greatest weightlifting deed ever when he lifted 6000 pounds.
 a. acted
 b. made or did

Check your answers. You should have picked **b** for 1, **a** for 2, **a** for 3, and **b** for 4.

C. Here are the kinds of questions you sometimes see on a reading test. Read the meaning printed at the top of the question. Then find the sentence in which the word in dark type has the same meaning. Put your answers on your paper.

1. quick or speedy
 a. The **fleet** runner set a new record.
 b. A **fleet** of ships arrived in the harbor.

2. not wear out
 a. A good pair of shoes should **last** several years.
 b. The **last** pair of shoes I bought are two years old.

3. is very angry
 a. My brother **fumes** when I wear his clothes.
 b. The **fumes** from the garbage are very strong.

4. clever or smart
 a. The knife had a very **keen** edge.
 b. Hector has a very **keen** mind.

5. lose weight
 a. Anton hopes he will **reduce** on his diet.
 b. The President hopes to **reduce** taxes.

6. a move or change
 a. Bonita is working the early **shift** at the restaurant.
 b. The boss announced a **shift** in the rules.

Check your answers. You should have picked **a** for 1, **a** for 2, **a** for 3, **b** for 4, **a** for 5, and **b** for 6.

LESSON 1

Here are the eight new words in this lesson. Their meanings are not listed. Each new word has several different meanings. Look for each word in the story. Use context clues to help you guess the meaning that fits in the story.

trial	**admitted**
case	**deed**
serve	**sentences**
handle	**just**

Teenage Juries

Have you ever been to a **trial**? You might get to be part of a trial someday soon. You won't be in court because you have broken the law. Instead, you could be one of the jury that decides a **case**.

Since 1978, teenagers have been able to **serve** on special juries in Duluth, Minnesota. Each jury is made up of high school students. They **handle** the cases of other young people who have broken the law.

The lawbreakers who appear before a teen jury have already **admitted** their crimes. The teen jury decides only the punishment for each wrong **deed**. Cases may involve stealing, fighting, harming property, using drugs, or drinking.

A teen jury can't put anyone in jail. But it can give out other **sentences**. Lawbreakers may have to write letters of apology. They may be told to do helpful work in their neighborhoods. They may also have to pay for any damages they caused.

Teen juries need to act carefully. They must make sure each sentence they give out is **just**. They also must keep their work a secret. Even lawbreakers have a right to be protected.

So far, teen courts have worked well in Duluth. Now other cities are trying them, too.

A. Each of the words in Lesson 1 is listed below. After each word are two of its meanings. Decide which meaning fits the way the word was used in the story on page 132. Put your answers on your paper.

1. trial
  a. a test
  b. a court case

2. case
  a. problem brought to court
  b. a box or container

3. serve
  a. bring food to
  b. do work for

4. handle
  a. something you hold
  b. deal with

5. admitted
  a. let someone come in
  b. said something was true or confessed

6. deed
  a. an act someone did
  b. a paper that shows that someone owns land

7. sentences
  a. decisions or judgments
  b. groups of words

8. just
  a. only
  b. fair or right

B. The words below mean the same as four new words in this lesson. Match each word with a lesson word. Put your answers on your paper.

1. judgments
2. act

3. fair
4. confessed

C. Write a sentence to answer each question below. Use the lesson word in dark type in your sentence.

1. What hard problem did you once have to **handle**?
2. What people have made the news lately by being on **trial**?
3. What is one reason you would like to **serve** on a teen jury?

Here are the eight new words in this lesson. Their meanings are not listed. Each new word has several different meanings. Look for each word in the story. Use context clues to help you guess the meaning that fits in the story.

elected	**cast**
run	**term**
office	**view**
platform	**sole**

A Woman Who Stood Alone

In 1916, Jeannette Rankin was **elected** to the U.S. Congress. She became the first woman ever to serve in Congress. Many people had been surprised to see a woman **run** for Congress. In many parts of the country women were not even allowed to vote. People were even more surprised to learn that Rankin had won the **office**.

Rankin believed strongly in women's rights. She also believed in peace. Her winning **platform** was based on these two ideas.

Later, Rankin showed just how strongly she believed in peace. In 1917, Congress voted for the U.S. to fight in World War I. Rankin was the only person in Congress who **cast** a vote against fighting.

Rankin lost when she ran for the next **term** of Congress. Her **view** on the war had turned many voters against her.

Rankin showed she was not a person who gave up easily. She finally won a second term many years later—in 1941. That year, Congress voted for the U.S. to fight in World War II. Rankin again became the **sole** member of Congress who voted against joining in the war.

A. Each of the words in Lesson 2 is listed below. After each word are two of its meanings. Decide which meaning fits the way the word was used in the story on page 134. Put your answers on your paper.

1. **elected**
   a. chose
   b. voted into office

2. **run**
   a. move quickly
   b. be in an election

3. **office**
   a. a job or position
   b. a place of work

4. **platform**
   a. ideas you speak out for
   b. raised floor or stage

5. **cast**
   a. people in a play
   b. put in

6. **term**
   a. a set period of time
   b. a special word or phrase

7. **view**
   a. an opinion or belief
   b. something that you see

8. **sole**
   a. bottom of the foot
   b. the one and only

B. The words below mean the same as four new words in this lesson. Match each word with a lesson word. Put your answers on your paper.

1. opinion
2. only
3. position
4. time period

C. Write a sentence to answer each question below. Use the lesson word in dark type in your sentence.

1. Who do you think will be **elected** President next time?
2. Who would you have **cast** your vote for in the last election for President?
3. How long is the **term** of a U.S. President?

LESSON 3

Here are the eight new words in this lesson. Their meanings are not listed. Each new word has several different meanings. Look for each word in the story below. Use context clues to help you guess the meaning that fits in the story.

devices	**composition**
inclined	**novel**
coat	**store**
finish	**fashion**

A House That Cleans Itself

Frances Gabe is a woman who does not like to clean her house. She feels it is a waste of time to wash, sweep, and dust. Gabe has found a better way. She lets the house clean itself.

Gabe is a builder and inventor. She has built a house in Oregon with many special **devices**. All she does is press buttons. The floors and walls are sprayed with soap and water. So are the doors and windows. The floors are **inclined**, so water runs off at the corners. Blowers then dry everything.

Water doesn't harm anything in the house. The floors and walls have a **coat** of resin on them. This **finish** keeps water from soaking in. The furniture is made of a special washable **composition** that Gabe invented.

Gabe also has a **novel** way of doing dishes. Most people put dishes in a sink or washer. Later, they take them out and **store** them in a cupboard. Gabe has built a cupboard that washes the dishes and saves time.

Clothes are cleaned in a similar **fashion**. They are washed and dried while they hang in the closet.

In fact everything in the house can be cleaned by pushing a button. This includes the sink, tub, shower, fireplace—even the dogs and cats.

A. Each of the words in Lesson 3 is listed on the next page. After each word are two of its meanings. Decide which meaning fits the way the word was used in this story. Put your answer on your paper.

1. devices
   a. tricks
   b. tools or inventions

2. inclined
   a. leaning or slanted
   b. feeling a certain way

3. coat
   a. an item of clothing
   b. a layer or covering

4. finish
   a. end or complete
   b. a final covering

5. composition
   a. a mixture of materials
   b. a piece of writing

6. novel
   a. new or unusual
   b. a fiction book

7. store
   a. a place to buy things
   b. keep somewhere

8. fashion
   a. a way of doing things
   b. a style of clothing

B. The words below mean the same as four new words in this lesson. Match each word with a lesson word. Put your answers on your paper.

1. mixture
2. way

3. new
4. slanted

C. Write a sentence to answer each question below. Use the lesson word in dark type in your sentence.

1. Where do you **store** your books in school?
2. What are some time-saving **devices** you have in your home?
3. How many **coats** of paint does it usually take to cover a wall completely?

Choose the word or phrase that means the same, or almost the same, as each word in dark type. Put your answers on your answer sheet.

Test Tip: Remember that some words have several different meanings. Think of the different meanings of each word in dark type. Look for one of the meanings in the list of answers.

1. a **trial** run
   a. fast
   b. test
   c. winning
   d. fair

2. a **novel** idea
   a. wonderful
   b. untrue
   c. new
   d. deep

3. political **views**
   a. opinions
   b. elections
   c. parties
   d. offices

4. **finish** that protects
   a. ending
   b. covering
   c. water
   d. guard

5. court **sentences**
   a. laws
   b. cases
   c. judgments
   d. words

6. a similar **fashion**
   a. cloth
   b. way
   c. opinion
   d. same

7. **sole** survivor
   a. only
   b. living
   c. solid
   d. saved

8. helpful **devices**
   a. ideas
   b. inventions
   c. people
   d. hints

Choose the sentence in which the word in dark type means the same as the definition given.

Test Tip: Remember that the same word can have several different meanings. Look at the way the word in dark type is used in each sentence. Pick the sentence in which the word in dark type means the same as the definition given. Don't be confused by other meanings of the word.

1. mixture of materials
   a. Orange paint is a **composition** of red and yellow paints.
   b. Jack wrote an award-winning **composition**.
   c. The band played a **composition** by John Philip Sousa.

2. fair
   a. I have **just** 25 cents in my pocket.
   b. We arrived **just** in time to see the parade.
   c. Everyone thought that the teacher's decision was **just**.

3. job or position
   a. Jean Geary decided to run for the **office** of mayor.
   b. A new **office** building is currently being built.
   c. The dentist has set up an **office** in his house.

4. confessed
   a. The criminal **admitted** that he stole the purse.
   b. Only 250 people can be **admitted** to the dance.
   c. The lawyer **admitted** the woman into his office.

5. ideas you speak out for
   a. Arthur gave his speech from a **platform** in front.
   b. The governor announced his new **platform**.
   c. **Platform** shoes can be very dangerous to walk in.

6. keep things somewhere
   a. I prefer to shop in a small **store**.
   b. I have a huge **store** of records in my den.
   c. You should not **store** bananas in a refrigerator.

In Part 4, you are going to learn another good way to guess what a new word means. Sometimes part of a new word will be a word you already know. You will learn to look for word parts and to use them as clues to the meaning of new words.

Look at the two pictures below. One picture shows the meaning of the word **highland**. The other picture shows the meaning of the word **crossroad**. Can you match each picture with the right word? Can you guess the meaning of each new word?

Sometimes you will see a new word in your reading or on a vocabulary test. You notice that a word you already know is part of the new word. Many times you can use the word inside to help you guess what the new word means. This trick does not always work. But it can help you sometimes.

Another way that you can use word parts is by looking at word endings. The ending of a word can give you a clue to its meaning. One ending you often see on words is *less*. The words *joyless, hopeless,* and *thoughtless* all have this ending. The ending *less* means *not having any* or *without*. So *joyless* means *without joy*. What would *hopeless* mean?

Read the following paragraph about a strange car that people once used. Two words are printed in dark type in the paragraph. Use parts of each new word to help you guess its meaning.

A car called the Haynes was built in 1898. It was very **comical** looking. Its builder had attached a stuffed horse's head to the front of the car. The head was supposed to make horses think the car was just another horse. But the head was **useless** in stopping horses from being frightened by the car.

1. What word do you see inside **comical**? That word can help you guess that **comical** means __.
   a. strange
   b. funny

2. What word do you see inside **useless**? What ending does **useless** have? The inside word and the ending can help you guess that **useless** means __.
   a. without use
   b. having many uses

Check your answers. The correct answers are **b** for 1 and **a** for 2.

Do the activities on the next two pages. You will learn more about using word parts to help you guess a new word's meaning.

A. Look at the words in List 1 below. Try to find words you already know inside the new words. Then look at the meanings in List 2. Try to match each word with its meaning. Put your answers on your paper.

LIST 1
1. tireless
2. silversmith
3. greenhouse
4. soundless
5. seagoing

LIST 2
a. made for sailing
b. without getting tired
c. someone who makes things from silver
d. building for growing plants
e. quiet

Check your answers. Correct matches are **b** for 1, **c** for 2, **d** for 3, **e** for 4, and **a** for 5.

B. Read the following paragraph about another strange car. Look for word parts in the words in dark type. Then answer the questions. Put your answers on your paper.

A **handmade** car, built in 1906, looked like it was part machine and part horse. The car had wheels in the front but not in the back. Two iron "horse" legs held the car up in the back and helped it move. The legs were driven by a chain, just as a bicycle tire is. The legs **enabled** the car to get around in an **effortless** way on wet or **ice-coated** roads.

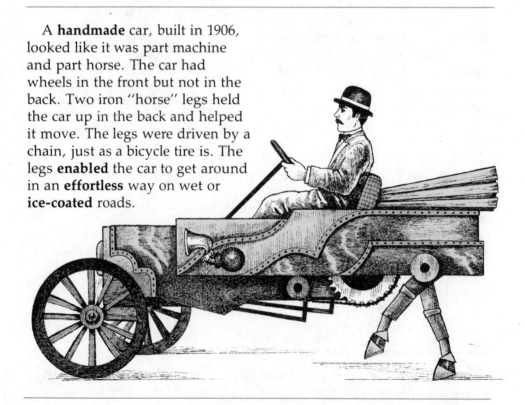

142

1. Which word means *made something able*?
2. Which word means *without any effort*?
3. Which word means *built by hand and not by machine*?
4. Which word means *covered with ice*?

Check your answers. Your answers should be 1. enabled, 2. effortless, 3. handmade, and 4. ice-coated.

C. Here are the kinds of questions you sometimes see on reading tests. Read the beginning of each question. Then find the answer that best completes the sentence. Use word parts to help you choose the answers. Put your answers on your paper.

1. A fearless person is someone who is __.
   a. afraid
   b. not afraid
   c. scary

2. People who buy farmland usually plan to __.
   a. build houses on it
   b. hunt animals on it
   c. grow crops on it

3. A painting that is worthless is __.
   a. not valuable
   b. valuable
   c. beautiful

4. Someone who thinks cleanliness is important __.
   a. hates to wash things
   b. likes to be clean
   c. is very kind

5. If you overtake someone in a race, you __.
   a. fall behind
   b. go ahead
   c. lose

6. If you receive payment for something you did, you __.
   a. buy something
   b. pay someone
   c. get paid

Check your answers. You should have picked **b** for 1, **c** for 2, **a** for 3, **b** for 4, **b** for 5, and **c** for 6.

LESSON 1

Here are the eight new words in this lesson. Their meanings are not listed. Notice how the words are used in the story below. Look for a word you know inside each new word. The words inside will help you guess the meanings of the new words.

wondrous	**errorless**
examine	**worldwide**
questioning	**predictions**
speechless	**peacefulness**

A Mind-Reading Horse

Lady Wonder was a horse that lived up to her name. She could do **wondrous** things. Lady Wonder could spell, type, and answer questions. Some people think she could even read minds.

In 1927, Lady's owner Claudine Fonda told people her horse could spell. Dr. J.B. Rhine came to **examine** the horse. He found Lady inside her stable. She had a set of alphabet blocks on a table in front of her.

Dr. Rhine began **questioning** Lady. He asked, "What is my name?" Lady touched the blocks R-H-I-N-E with her nose. Next Rhine asked, "Where can I borrow money?" Lady touched the blocks B-A-N-K.

Dr. Rhine was so surprised that he was **speechless**. He asked more questions. He even asked Lady to answer math problems. Her answers were **errorless**.

Lady Wonder soon gained **worldwide** attention. People came from all over to ask her questions. A special typewriter was built for Lady to use. In 1948, Lady typed out some **predictions** about the future. She said there would be two more years of **peacefulness**. Then a war would start. Lady was right. The Korean War began in 1950. Lady also told police where to find missing people.

Lady made a few mistakes. But she was right 95% of the time. She died in 1957 when she was 33. No one ever learned the secret of her powers.

A. Look for words you already know inside the new words on page 144. The words inside will help you pick the best meanings in the questions below. Put your answers on your paper.

1. What word is almost spelled out inside **wondrous**? That word will help you guess that **wondrous** means ___.
   a. normal
   b. marvelous
   c. winning

2. What word do you see inside **examine**? That word helps you guess that **examine** means ___.
   a. see
   b. mind
   c. test

3. What word do you see inside **questioning**? That word helps you guess that **questioning** means ___.
   a. answering
   b. asking questions
   c. testing

4. What word do you see inside **speechless**? What ending do you see? You can guess that **speechless** means ___.
   a. not able to talk
   b. not able to hear
   c. not able to see

5. What word do you see inside **errorless**? What ending do you see? You can guess that **errorless** means ___.
   a. wrong
   b. amazing
   c. correct

6. What words do you see inside **worldwide**? Those words help you guess that **worldwide** means ___.
   a. all over the world
   b. all over the country
   c. very wide

7. What word do you see inside **predictions**? That word helps you guess that **predictions** means ___.
   a. words
   b. names
   c. forecasts

8. What word do you see inside **peacefulness**? That word helps you guess that **peacefulness** means ___.
   a. wartime
   b. peacetime
   c. fighting

B. Write a sentence to answer each question below. Use the lesson word in dark type in your sentence.

1. If your math test is **errorless**, what grade should you make?
2. What is the name of one person who is famous **worldwide**?
3. What is one **wondrous** thing that you have seen someone do?

LESSON 2

Here are the eight new words in this lesson. Their meanings are not listed. Notice how the words are used in the story below. Look for a word you know inside each new word. The words inside will help you guess the meanings of the new words.

motionless   **advertised**
lifelike   **performances**
youngster   **comedians**
repeatedly   **talkative**

Willie Tyler and Lester

When Willie Tyler and his friend Lester get together, Willie does all the talking. Anybody listening to them would hear two voices, however. That is because Willie is a ventriloquist. Lester is Willie's wooden ventriloquist's figure. Willie can keep his lips **motionless** and still make sounds that seem to come out of Lester's mouth. Lester's face and voice seem so **lifelike** that people believe he is really talking.

Willie first tried ventriloquism when he was a **youngster** in Detroit. He practiced with one of his sister's dolls. He would speak sentences **repeatedly** in front of a mirror, making sure his lips didn't move. Soon he decided to buy his first figure. He wanted a black figure, but all the ones **advertised** were white. He bought a white one and painted it.

When Willie was 12 he saw a black figure in a catalog and ordered it. The figure was his first Lester. He has bought several more Lesters since that time.

Willie and Lester give many **performances** every year on TV or on stage. They are **comedians** and singers. They work well together. Willie says they get along so well because they are opposites. Willie is quiet and Lester is **talkative**.

Many ventriloquists call their partners "dummies." Why does Willie call Lester a "ventriloquist's figure" instead? Lester answers that question. "You wouldn't want to hurt the feelings of a little wooden dude!" he says.

A. Look for words you already know inside the new words on page 146. The words inside will help you pick the best meanings in the questions below. Put your answers on your paper.

1. What word do you see inside **motionless**? What ending do you see? You can guess that **motionless** means ___.
   a. moving
   b. without moving
   c. together

2. What words do you see inside **lifelike**? Those words help you guess that **lifelike** means ___.
   a. like real life
   b. friendly
   c. old

3. What word do you see inside **youngster**? That word helps you guess **youngster** means ___.
   a. man
   b. person
   c. child

4. What word do you see inside **repeatedly**? That word helps you guess **repeatedly** means ___.
   a. sometimes
   b. over and over
   c. not very often

5. What word do you see inside **advertised**? That word helps you guess **advertised** means ___.
   a. offered in ads
   b. realized
   c. bought

6. What word do you see inside **performances**? That word helps you guess **performances** means ___.
   a. talks
   b. acts or shows
   c. thoughts

7. What word is almost spelled out in **comedians**? That word helps you guess **comedians** means ___.
   a. people who sing
   b. people who dance
   c. people who tell jokes

8. What word do you see inside **talkative**? That word helps you guess that **talkative** means ___.
   a. noisy
   b. quiet
   c. happy

B. Write a sentence to answer each question below. Use the lesson word in dark type in your sentence.

1. Why is it hard to remain **motionless** for a long time?
2. What is one thing that you have practiced **repeatedly**?
3. What stores often **advertise** in your town's newspaper?

TAKING TESTS

Choose the word or phrase that best completes each sentence. Put your answers on your answer sheet.

Test Tips: This kind of question asks you to think about the meaning of the key word. Then you need to use the meaning to choose the best answer. Read the sentences carefully. Use word parts to help you guess the meanings of the key words.

---

1. A talkative person is almost never __.
   a. standing still
   b. talking
   c. quiet
   d. unhappy

2. Someone who is famous worldwide is well-known __.
   a. to a few people
   b. to a lot of people
   c. only in the U.S.
   d. only in Europe

3. In a time of peacefulness there are no __.
   a. wars
   b. friends
   c. happy people
   d. soldiers

4. Predictions are guesses made about __.
   a. the past
   b. wars
   c. the future
   d. missing people

5. Something that is lifelike seems to be __.
   a. strange
   b. unusual
   c. funny
   d. real

6. When you examine something you usually __.
   a. laugh
   b. become frightened
   c. study it carefully
   d. keep your eyes closed

UNIT III
STUDY SKILLS

You can get the facts in many different ways:

A. By reading a passage.

Spain is almost twice the size of Italy. Italy is more than twice the size of Greece. And Italy is three times the size of Portugal.

B. By looking at maps. (Maps are drawings of parts of the Earth.)

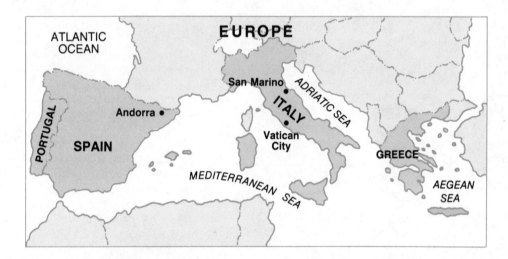

C. By reading a chart called a table. (A table is a list of facts that can be read quickly.)

SIZES OF COUNTRIES	
Country	Area (in square miles)
Greece	50,547
Italy	116,303
Portugal	35,340
Spain	194,883

D. By looking at a graph where the facts really stand out.

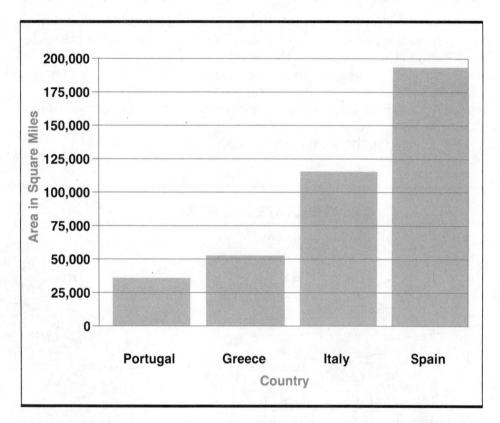

Read the questions below. They are based on one of the visual materials you just studied. Try to answer the question before you study the choices. Write your answers on your paper.

1. Which visual material tells the exact size of Spain?
  a. passage   c. table
  b. map   d. graph

2. Which visual material shows that Portugal and Spain are neighbors?
  a. passage   c. table
  b. map   d. graph

3. Which visual material best shows at a glance that Spain is almost four times bigger than Greece?
  a. passage   c. table
  b. map   d. graph

LESSON 1

Thirteen States

On June 21, 1788, New Hampshire made U.S. history. On that day New Hampshire became the ninth state to vote for the United States Constitution. There were only 13 states then. And only nine were needed for the Constitution to become the law of our land. It was not easy for the 13 states to decide on this. New Hampshire took over a year to decide. Four other states took even longer. In fact, Rhode Island was the last one to decide in 1790.

Here is a map of the United States. Can you find the original 13 states?

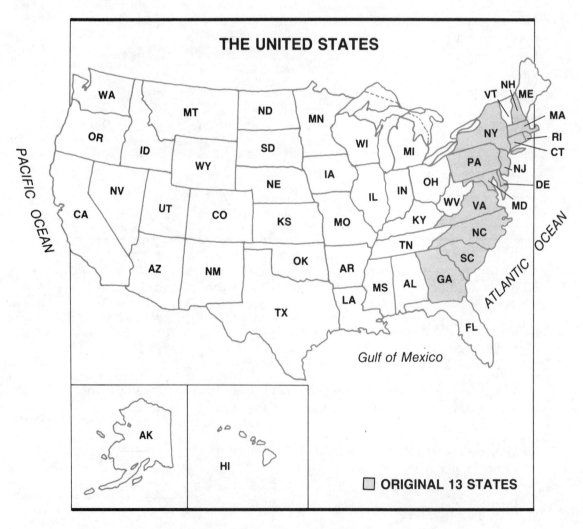

THE UNITED STATES

☐ **ORIGINAL 13 STATES**

Maps are flat drawings of the whole Earth or parts of it. The map on the left shows the shapes and sizes of the 50 states. Like most U.S. maps, the names of the states are abbreviated. The states that are shaded are the original 13 states.

Choose the best answer.

1. Which of these states was one of the original 13?
   a. Indiana
   b. Vermont
   c. Maine
   d. New York

Check your answer. Of these four states, only New York is shaded. It has the abbreviation NY on it. The answer is **d**.

2. Which of these states was not one of the original 13?
   a. Maryland
   b. Utah
   c. Georgia
   d. New Jersey

3. The first state to vote for the Constitution was a small state. It is just below Pennsylvania. The state is __.
   a. West Virginia
   b. Delaware
   c. Virginia
   d. Connecticut

4. Which of the 13 original states does not touch the Atlantic Ocean?
   a. South Carolina
   b. Pennsylvania
   c. Virginia
   d. Delaware

5. Which state has Nevada on one side and the Pacific Ocean on the other?
   a. California
   b. Utah
   c. Washington
   d. Maine

6. Two states on the Atlantic Ocean were not in the original 13. These states are __.
   a. West Virginia and Virginia
   b. Maine and Florida
   c. Vermont and Maine
   d. Oregon and Florida

LESSON 2

The Solar Challenger

Fly a plane without fuel? Impossible? Not for the Solar Challenger. On a bright, sunny day, the plane took off but it soon fell back to the ground. The pilot tried again and again. On the eighth try, the plane was up and on its way.

The pilot headed from Cormeilles en Vexin, France, to the English Channel. Five and a half hours later, he landed at Manston Royal Air Force Base. That's near Dover in England. The date was July 7, 1981. The Solar Challenger had crossed the English Channel using only the rays of the sun for power.

The map below shows the route the Solar Challenger took.

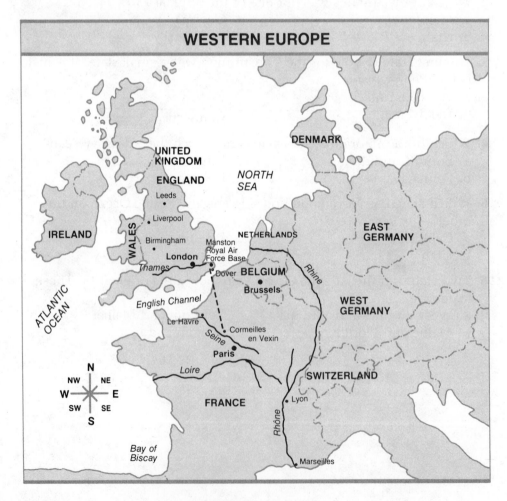

154

To follow the path of the Solar Challenger on a map, you must be able to find directions. The main directions on a map are north (N), south (S), east (E), and west (W). Between them are four "halfway" directions. They are northeast (NE), northwest (NW), southeast (SE), and southwest (SW). You will find these directions on a map's compass rose. Find the compass rose in the lower left corner of the map.

Some maps use only an arrow pointing north. When you know which direction is north, you can figure out that south is below. West is to the left. East is to the right.

Choose the best answer.

1. From Cormeilles en Vexin to the English Channel, the pilot had to fly __.
   a. northwest   c. southwest
   b. northeast   d. southeast

Check your answer. The English Channel is above Cormeilles en Vexin on the map. The answer is **a**.

2. Dover is near the __ coast of England.
   a. northeastern   c. southeastern
   b. northwestern   d. southwestern

3. What city is northeast of Cormeilles en Vexin?
   a. Marseilles   c. Lyon
   b. Brussels   d. Birmingham

4. From Dover, the direction to Liverpool is __.
   a. NE   c. NW
   b. SE   d. SW

5. If you fly from London to Brussels, you are traveling __.
   a. east to west   c. north to south
   b. west to east   d. south to north

6. If the pilot had flown east from Cormeilles en Vexin, where might he have landed?
   a. West Germany   c. Ireland
   b. Denmark   d. Belgium

Stop That River

How do you stop a river from moving? Well, that's just what the Army is trying to do. It all started because part of the Mississippi River seems to be changing its path. So the Army is building up the soil on both sides of the river. It is hoped that this will stop the river from moving.

The people of New Orleans are also hoping that the river does not move. The map of Louisiana shows why. If the river changes its path, New Orleans will be left without a water supply.

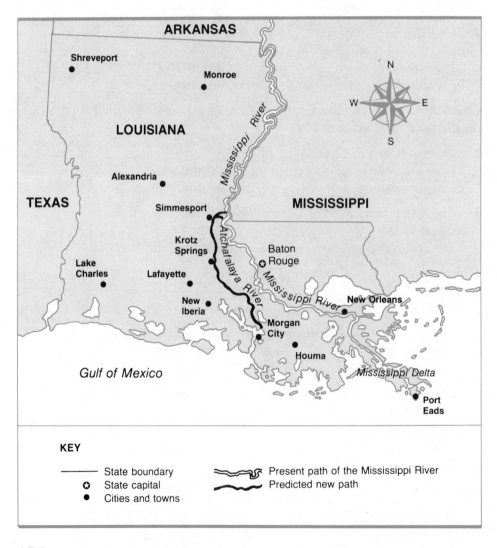

At the bottom of the map of Louisiana is a map key. The key shows you the symbols used on the map. Each symbol stands for something on the map such as cities, towns, and the path of the river. Use the map and the map key to answer the questions.

Choose the best answer.

1. What state capital is on the Mississippi River?
    a. Shreveport   c. New Orleans
    b. Baton Rouge   d. Morgan City

Check your answer. The symbol for the state capital is ★. So, the answer is **b.**

2. Which city is on the Mississippi River?
    a. Morgan City   c. New Orleans
    b. Krotz Springs   d. Houma

3. Which two towns would be on the new path if the river moves?
    a. New Orleans and Houma   c. Port Eads and New Orleans
    b. Simmesport and Houma   d. Simmesport and Krotz Springs

4. What state is west of the Mississippi River?
    a. Louisiana   c. Mississippi
    b. Alabama   d. Florida

5. If the Mississippi River moves, the new path will be ___ of the present path.
    a. west   c. north
    b. east   d. south

6. The Mississippi River is the state boundary between two states. They are ___.
    a. Louisiana and Arkansas   c. Texas and Louisiana
    b. Mississippi and Texas   d. Mississippi and Louisiana

A Serious Game

Think how exciting the final game of the World Series is. Or the Super Bowl. That's how many people around the world feel about soccer games. Soccer is a very serious sport. They say that two countries once started a war because of a soccer game! For that reason, many stadiums try to keep players and fans apart. Some stadiums have high wire fences around the playing field. Others have deep water moats to keep the players away from unhappy fans.

Most Americans don't take soccer that seriously. But soccer is becoming more and more popular in America. There are more new teams and new fans each season. Look at the August calendar below to find out when the Blue Stars are playing.

AUGUST 1983

SUN.	MON.	TUES.	WED.	THURS.	FRI.	SAT.
	1	2	3	4	5	6
7 BLUE STARS & CHIEFS Home Game 2:30 p.m.	8	9	10 BLUE STARS & ROWDIES Home Game 7:30 p.m.	11	12	13
14 BLUE STARS & WHITECAPS Away Game 7:30 p.m.	15	16	17	18 BLUE STARS & WILD CATS Away Game 8:00 p.m.	19	20
21 BLUE STARS & ROWDIES Away Game 2:45 p.m.	22	23	24	25	26	27 BLUE STARS & KICKS Home Game 2:30 p.m.
28	29	30 BLUE STARS & WILD CATS Home Game 7:30 p.m.	31			

A calendar is a kind of table. The dates and days of the week are in columns and rows. A column goes up and down. A row goes from side to side. All the dates in one column fall on the same day of the week. All the dates in one row are in the same week.

Use the August calendar to answer the questions below.

Choose the best answer.

1. On what day of the week do the Blue Stars play the most games?
a. Sunday
c. Wednesday
b. Monday
d. Saturday

Check your answer. The column under Sunday has the most games listed. The answer is **a**.

2. If you want to go to a Tuesday night home game, who will the Blue Stars be playing?
a. the Rowdies
c. the Chiefs
b. the Kicks
d. the Wild Cats

3. On what date is the game between the Whitecaps and the Blue Stars?
a. the 7th
c. the 18th
b. the 14th
d. the 30th

4. No games will be played during the week of ___.
a. July 31–August 6
c. August 7–August 13
b. August 21–August 27
d. August 28–September 3

5. The Blue Stars play a home game on August 10th with the Rowdies. When is the next home game?
a. the 14th
c. the 27th
b. the 18th
d. the 30th

6. How many home games do the Blue Stars play in the first three weeks of August?
a. 4
c. 3
b. 2
d. 6

LESSON 5

Button Up Your Overcoat

The radio said it was going to be 35°F today. So you put your coat on. But you leave your hat and gloves at home. You go outside thinking it will be cold. But not too cold. And you find it's freezing out there. What happened? Did you forget the wind chill? The wind can make it seem colder than it really is. The wind and temperature together is what you have to keep in mind.

Look at the table below. It shows how the wind can make the temperature feel colder than it is.

WIND CHILL TABLE								
Actual Temperature (°F)	Wind Speed (miles per hour)							
	5	10	15	20	25	30	35	40
35	33	22	16	12	8	6	4	3
30	27	16	9	4	1	−2	−4	−5
25	21	10	2	−3	−7	−10	−12	−13
20	19	3	−5	−10	−15	−18	−20	−21
15	12	−3	−11	−17	−22	−25	−27	−29
10	7	−9	−18	−24	−29	−33	−35	−37
5	0	−15	−25	−31	−36	−41	−43	−45
0	−5	−22	−31	−39	−44	−49	−52	−53

How do you read the table? Suppose its 25°F outside and the wind is blowing at 20 miles per hour. Run your finger down the list of temperatures to find 25°F. Next run your other finger across the list of wind speeds until you find 20 miles per hour. Now move the finger on the temperature to the right. Move the finger on the wind speed down. Where do they meet? That's how cold it feels. Now you can decide how many sweaters to put on.

Choose the best answer.

1. It's 15°F outside and the wind is blowing at 10 miles per hour. It feels like ___.
   a. −3°F
   b. −11°F
   c. 11°F
   d. 15°F

Check your answer. Your fingers meet at −3°F. The answer is **a.**

2. The wind is blowing 15 miles per hour. The temperature is 20°F. The wind chill makes it feel like ___.
   a. −5°F
   b. −17°F
   c. 19°F
   d. 16°F

3. The temperature is 35°F but it feels like 6°F outside. How fast is the wind blowing?
   a. 5 miles per hour
   b. 15 miles per hour
   c. 30 miles per hour
   d. 40 miles per hour

4. The wind chill makes it feel like 0°. The wind is blowing 5 miles per hour. What is the temperature?
   a. 10°F
   b. −5°F
   c. 0°F
   d. 5°F

5. When would you feel the warmest?
   a. 30°F and the wind speed is 15 miles per hour
   b. 25°F and the wind speed is 25 miles per hour
   c. 20°F and the wind speed is 5 miles per hour
   d. 10°F and the wind speed is 5 miles per hour

6. It's 25°F with a wind speed of 30 miles per hour. Which would feel as cold?
   a. 30°F and a wind speed of 25 miles per hour
   b. 25°F and a wind speed of 10 miles per hour
   c. 20°F and a wind speed of 20 miles per hour
   d. 5°F and a wind speed of 5 miles per hour

Going by Train

In a hurry? You could take a plane. But wait a minute. Some new trains move so fast that you can take a train and get there almost as quickly.

Some of Japan's trains can travel up to 130 miles per hour. The trains run on electricity. The ride is fast and quiet. And the trains run on time. In fact, people only get two minutes to get in and out of the train before the doors close.

The Japanese are working on a new train. This one will be able to travel at 340 miles per hour! Find out about other fast trains by looking at the table below.

FASTEST PASSENGER-TRAIN RUNS			
Train	Country	Distance of Trip (miles)	Speed (miles per hour)
Hikari	Japan	196	112
Southwest Limited	USA	100	82
TGV train	France	40	118
Turbotrain	Canada	311	83
High Speed train	England	112	104

The table is arranged in columns and rows. A column goes up and down. Each column has a title. The title tells what kinds of facts are in the column. All the words in the first column are the names of the trains.

A row in a table goes across from side to side. Each row has facts about the train named in the first column. One fact about the Hikari is that it can go 112 miles per hour.

Use the table to answer the questions below.

Choose the best answer.

1. What country has a train that can go almost 105 miles per hour?
   a. England
   b. USA
   c. France
   d. Japan

Check your answer. Find the speed that is almost 105 miles per hour. Find the country in the same row. The answer is **a**.

2. Which train travels the longest distance?
   a. Hikari
   b. Turbotrain
   c. High Speed train
   d. TGV train

3. Which country has a train that is faster than the Hikari?
   a. USA
   b. England
   c. Japan
   d. France

4. Which two trains travel at about the same speed?
   a. Southwest Limited and TGV train
   b. TGV train and High Speed train
   c. Hikari and Turbotrain
   d. Southwest Limited and Turbotrain

5. How much faster does the TGV train travel than the Southwest Limited?
   a. 82 miles per hour
   b. 36 miles per hour
   c. 118 miles per hour
   d. 1 mile per hour

6. The fastest train travels ___.
   a. the longest distance
   b. the shortest distance
   c. 100 miles more than the others
   d. 100 miles less than the others

The Price of Honor

For the first time, two countries are using the same stamp. The countries are Ireland and the United States. Whose picture is on this stamp? James Hoban. Hoban was born in Ireland in 1762. He came to the U.S. in 1789. Hoban designed the White House.

The Hoban stamp is the same in both countries except for the name of the country and the price.

The Hoban stamp was supposed to cost 18¢ in the United States. But before the stamp was printed, the price of stamps went up. That was the second time in one year the price of stamps had gone up.

Look at the pictograph below. It shows how much the price of U.S. stamps has gone up since 1971.

COST OF A STAMP					
1981 (Nov.)	🏛️	🏛️	🏛️	🏛️	🏛️
1981 (March)	🏛️	🏛️	🏛️	🏛️	🏛️
1978	🏛️	🏛️	🏛️	🏛️	
1975	🏛️	🏛️	🏛️	🏛️	
1974	🏛️	🏛️	🏛️		
1971	🏛️	🏛️			

KEY = 4 cents

A pictograph uses pictures, or symbols, to show facts. In this pictograph, the symbol is a stamp. Find the key at the bottom of the graph. The key tells you that each stamp stands for four cents. A half-stamp is two cents, and so on.

To read the graph, count the number of stamps in the row for each year. A row runs across from side to side. Use the graph to answer the questions below.

Choose the best answer.

1. The cost of a James Hoban stamp in November of 1981 was ___.
   a. 4¢
   b. 5¢
   c. 18¢
   d. 20¢

Check your answer. There are 5 stamps in the row beside 1981 (November). Each stamp stands for 4 cents. The answer is **d**.

2. The price of a stamp from March 1981 to November 1981 went up by ___.
   a. 2¢
   b. 4¢
   c. 5¢
   d. 6¢

3. People spent 13¢ for each stamp in the year ___.
   a. 1971
   b. 1974
   c. 1975
   d. 1978

4. From 1971 to November 1981, the cost of stamps ___.
   a. went up by 12¢
   b. went down by 10¢
   c. doubled
   d. stayed the same

5. In 1974, a stamp cost 10¢. The cost of stamps had doubled by ___.
   a. November 1981
   b. March 1981
   c. 1978
   d. 1971

6. The cost of stamps went up the most from ___.
   a. 1971 to 1974
   b. 1974 to 1975
   c. 1975 to 1978
   d. 1978 to November 1981

The World's Tallest

What is the tallest building in the world? For many years it was the Empire State Building. But now the Empire State Building is only the third tallest building. And that may not be for very long either.

A new building in Chicago has been planned that will be 2,300 feet tall. That's almost 900 feet higher than any other building. It will have three times as much space inside as the Empire State Building.

Look at the bar graph below. It shows the height of the Empire State Building, the planned building, and other tall buildings in the world.

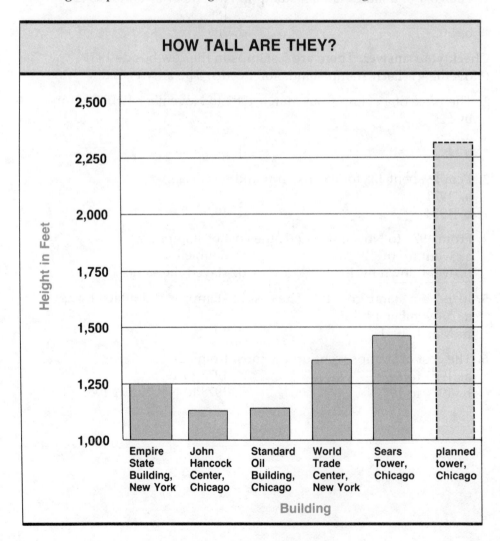

166

A bar graph has bars of different lengths, instead of pictures. This kind of graph makes it easy to compare things quickly. To read the graph, look where each bar ends. Then find the closest number at the side of the graph.

Use the bar graph to answer the questions below.

Choose the best answer.

1. What is the height of the Empire State Building?
    a. 1,000 feet   c. 1,350 feet
    b. 1,250 feet   d. 1,500 feet

Check your answer. The bar for the Empire State Building is exactly at 1,250 feet. The answer is **b**.

2. What building is the tallest building in the world at the present time?
    a. Empire State Building   c. Standard Oil Building
    b. World Trade Center   d. Sears Tower

3. One thousand three hundred and fifty feet is the height of the __.
    a. World Trade Center   c. Sears Tower
    b. John Hancock Center   d. Planned Tower

4. How much taller is the planned tower than the Empire State Building?
    a. about 1,000 feet   c. about 2,300 feet
    b. about 2,000 feet   d. more than 2,000 feet

5. The building closest in height to the Standard Oil Building is the __.
    a. Sears Tower   c. John Hancock Center
    b. World Trade Center   d. Empire State Building

6. The Sears Tower is about 100 feet taller than the __.
    a. planned tower   c. Empire State Building
    b. World Trade Center   d. Standard Oil Building

Saving the Whooping Crane

Would you think that taking an egg from a bird's nest would help it? Well, scientists are doing just that to the whooping crane. The whooping crane is a very rare bird. In fact, in 1941 there were only 15 whooping cranes in the whole world.

Something had to be done. The scientists had an idea. Whooping cranes lay two eggs. Usually only one chick lives. The scientists took one egg from the nest. Then they put the egg in an incubator. Or they had another bird hatch it. They hoped that both chicks might live.

It seems to have worked. By 1980 there were 78 whooping cranes living in the wild. The line graph below shows how the number of whooping cranes has grown since 1940.

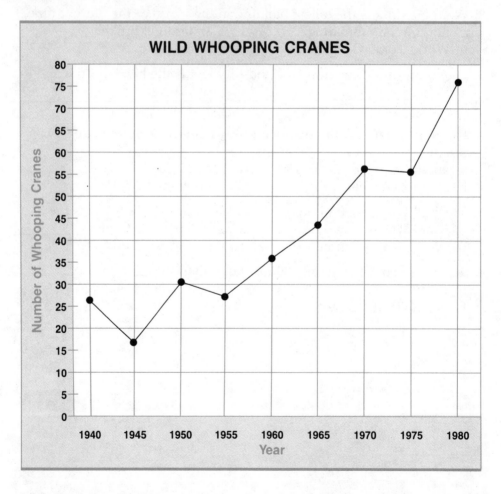

A line graph shows how something has changed. This kind of graph uses a simple line to show changes. If the line goes up, that means something has gone up. If the line goes down, then something has gone down.

Suppose you want to find out how many whooping cranes there were in the year 1970. Find 1970 at the bottom of the graph. Find the dot over that year. Then find the number of whooping cranes across from the dot.

Use the line graph to answer the questions below.

Choose the best answer.

1. How many whooping cranes were there in 1965?
  a. 40   c. 50
  b. 44   d. 65

Check your answer. The dot above 1965 is across from 44. The answer is **b**.

2. The line graph shows that the number of whooping cranes is __.
  a. going up   c. not changing
  b. going down   d. zero

3. What happened to the number of whooping cranes between the years 1945 and 1955?
  a. It went down and then up.   c. It went down and stayed down.
  b. It went up and then down.   d. It stayed the same.

4. Between which years did the number of whooping cranes stay about the same?
  a. 1950–1955   c. 1940–1945
  b. 1970–1975   d. 1975–1980

5. There were more than 40 but less than 50 whooping cranes in __.
  a. 1960   c. 1970
  b. 1965   d. 1975

6. How many more whooping cranes were there in 1980 than in 1950?
  a. 19   c. 31
  b. 55   d. 47

LESSON 10

How Do You Say It in Bemba?

Have you ever heard of a language called Bemba? It is spoken by two million people. Seems like a lot. Right? Well, Bemba doesn't even make it in the top 100 languages in the world. There are about 3,000 languages. Some of them, like French and German, are spoken by over 100 million people. And still they are not in the top five.

What are the five languages spoken by the most people in the world? Look at the pie graph below.

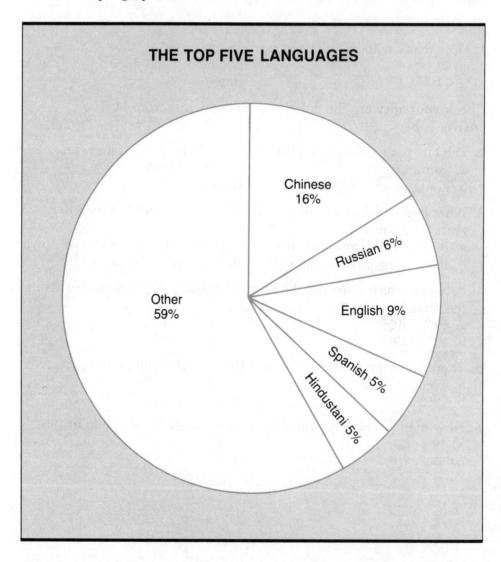

THE TOP FIVE LANGUAGES

Chinese 16%

Russian 6%

English 9%

Spanish 5%

Hindustani 5%

Other 59%

You can divide a pie into pieces of different sizes. That's also the idea of a pie graph, or circle graph. A pie graph shows how the whole is divided into parts.

The pie graph at the left has a number in each part. These numbers are percentages, or parts of 100 percent. All the numbers add up to 100%. Use the graph to answer the questions below.

Choose the best answer.

1. Which language is spoken by the most people?
   a. English
   b. Russian
   c. Spanish
   d. Chinese

Check your answer. Chinese has a bigger part in the pie graph than any of the other languages. The answer is **d**.

2. About the same number of people speak ___.
   a. Chinese and Hindustani
   b. English and Russian
   c. Spanish and Hindustani
   d. Spanish and English

3. More people speak Russian than ___.
   a. all the other languages
   b. Spanish
   c. Chinese
   d. English

4. The part marked *other* has the largest part of the circle because ___.
   a. more people speak other languages than Chinese
   b. more people speak Chinese than any other language
   c. many people speak more than one language
   d. everyone has one language they can speak better than any other

5. Together people who speak Chinese and English add up to what percentage of the world?
   a. 9%
   b. 16%
   c. 25%
   d. 59%

6. What percentage of the world speaks the five top languages?
   a. 41%
   b. 16%
   c. 50%
   d. 59%

TAKING TESTS

Sometimes, tests have questions that use visual materials such as maps, tables, and graphs. Use the visual materials as you follow the test tips on the next two pages. Put your answers on your answer sheet.

Test Tips: Know what each visual material does best. Some test questions ask which one you would use to get a certain kind of information.

Choose the best answer.

1. Where would you find the date of Thanksgiving Day this year?
   a. calendar   c. pictograph
   b. graph   d. map

2. Which one of these would answer the following question: "In what direction does the Mississippi River flow?"
   a. map   c. circle graph
   b. table   d. bar graph

3. Which one of these would best show how the average family spends its money?
   a. line graph   c. map
   b. circle graph   d. table

4. You must list the number of T-shirts in your store by size and color. Which visual material would you use?
   a. line graph   c. table
   b. circle graph   d. map

Test Tips: On a map reading test, the first thing to do is to study the map quickly. Study the symbols on the map key. Look at the compass rose. Read each question and try to answer it.

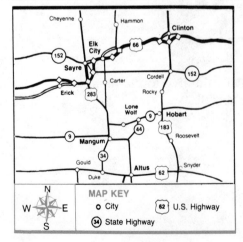

Choose the best answer.

5. Which city is east of Elk City?
   a. Sayre   c. Cordell
   b. Clinton   d. Hammon

6. Which highway would you take from Snyder to Clinton? What direction would you travel?
   a. 66, east   c. 183, north
   b. 62, west   d. 183, south

Test Tips: Some test questions are based on a graph. First, study each graph quickly. Then read each question. Be sure of your own answer. Check it on the graph.

Choose the best answer.

1. Which country on the bar graph has the least number of TV sets?
   a. Japan
   c. West Germany
   b. U.S.
   d. Great Britain

2. If the U.S. is number one in TV sets, what is the rank of the Soviet Union?
   a. first
   c. third
   b. second
   d. fourth

3. The line graph shows that since 1940, the value of a dollar has gone ___.
   a. steadily up
   b. down, then up
   c. steadily down
   d. up, then down

4. How much less could a dollar buy in 1980 than in 1967?
   a. about 25¢
   c. about 5¢
   b. about 90¢
   d. about 50¢

5. The circle graph shows that most of the energy we use comes from ___.
   a. wood
   c. coal
   b. oil
   d. water

6. More energy comes from water than from ___.
   a. oil
   c. natural gas
   b. coal
   d. sun

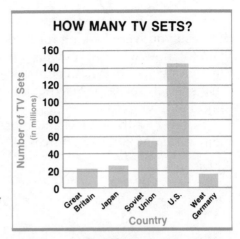

HOW MANY TV SETS?

Number of TV Sets (in millions)

Country: Great Britain, Japan, Soviet Union, U.S., West Germany

CHANGING VALUE OF A U.S. DOLLAR
(Based on 1967 Prices)

Value of a Dollar

1967

Year: 1930, 1940, 1950, 1960, 1970, 1980

Source: U.S. Bureau of Labor Statistics

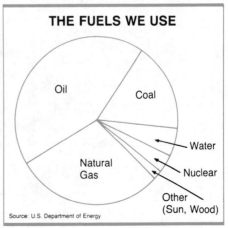

THE FUELS WE USE

Oil
Coal
Water
Natural Gas
Nuclear
Other (Sun, Wood)

Source: U.S. Department of Energy

Suppose you were looking for facts about the Olympics. You might want to know when and where the Olympics began. When will the next Olympics be held? What countries have the best Olympic records? Or what special words are used at Olympic events? And what sports are played at Olympic Games?

You can find these facts and more in reference materials. There are many different kinds of sources. These are some of them.

A. Dictionary

C. Almanac

B. Encyclopedia

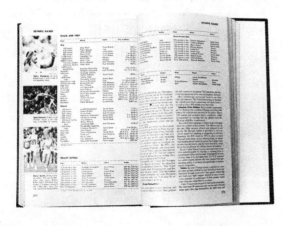

D. Books

E. Newspapers and Magazines

You don't have to read all these references to find the facts you need. You just have to know where to look. Do you know which one to use for what you need? Test yourself. Answer these questions.

Choose the best answer.

1. Which would you use to find the names of all track and field Olympic winners since 1896?
   a. dictionary   c. newspaper
   b. magazine   d. almanac

2. Which one would give the meaning of *Olympic*?
   a. dictionary   c. almanac
   b. sports book   d. newspaper

3. Which one would you use to find where the first Olympic Games were held?
   a. dictionary   c. encyclopedia
   b. newspaper   d. sports book

How do you find facts in each of these references? The next eight lessons will show you how.

LESSON 1

This Animal First

At night in a South African field, you might see a six-foot long earth pig. It does not look like most pigs, however. Its ears are too large. Its tail is too heavy and too long. It opens ant nests with powerful claws. It captures ants with its long and sticky tongue. Then it eats them. The animal you have just met is an aardvark.

Finding facts about the aardvark is easy. Thousands of animals are listed alphabetically in reference books. But the aardvark always comes first. The zebra and the zorilla probably appear last.

Below are sample entries in a reference book. Where would the aardvark be?

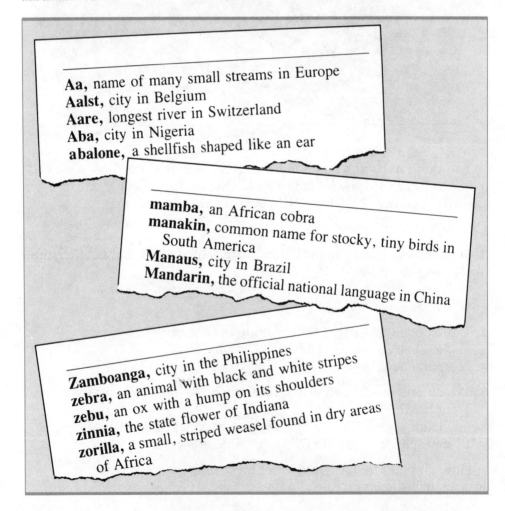

Aa, name of many small streams in Europe
Aalst, city in Belgium
Aare, longest river in Switzerland
Aba, city in Nigeria
abalone, a shellfish shaped like an ear

mamba, an African cobra
manakin, common name for stocky, tiny birds in South America
Manaus, city in Brazil
Mandarin, the official national language in China

Zamboanga, city in the Philippines
zebra, an animal with black and white stripes
zebu, an ox with a hump on its shoulders
zinnia, the state flower of Indiana
zorilla, a small, striped weasel found in dry areas of Africa

Entries in a reference book are listed alphabetically, from A to Z. When two words begin with the same letter, the second letter is used to decide the order. When the two beginning letters are the same, the third letter is used to decide the order, and so on.

Look at the entries on page 176 as you answer these questions.

Choose the best answer.

1. The aardvark may be the first animal, but it is not always the first entry. The aardvark will appear between ___.
   a. Aa and Aalst
   b. Aalst and Aare
   c. Aare and Aba
   d. Aba and abalone

Check your answer. The two beginning letters in the first three entries are the same. Look at the third and fourth letters. The answer is **b.**

2. The manatee is a large plant-eating animal that lives in water. It will be listed between ___.
   a. mamba and manakin
   b. Mandarin and the next entry
   c. Manaus and Mandarin
   d. manakin and Manaus

3. Where would facts about zealots be?
   a. between zebu and zinnia
   b. between zinnia and zorilla
   c. between Zamboanga and zebra
   d. between zebra and zebu

4. Where would you find the praying mantis?
   a. before manatee
   b. between man and manakin
   c. after Mandarin
   d. before mamba

5. In between which entries would kangaroo appear?
   a. kalimba, kamala
   b. kapok, karate
   c. kava, kayak
   d. kampong, kantele

6. Where would the flamingo appear?
   a. between flame tree and flank
   b. between flamen and flamenco
   c. before flamenco
   d. after flan

Teenager Becomes a Word

After the war in the 1940's there was a baby boom. More babies were born then than at any time in the U.S. These babies grew into young people in the 1950's. There were so many of them that a new word was made up for them. The word was *teenager*. It became a dictionary entry in the 1950's.

Suppose you have to find *teenager* quickly in your dictionary. How would you do it? Looking through all the words that begin with "t" may take a lot of time. Using the guide words at the top of each page will help.

Here are some guide words in a dictionary. On which page would the word *teenager* appear?

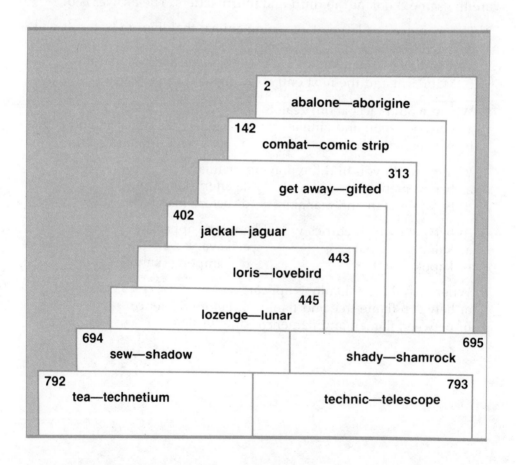

2
abalone—aborigine

142
combat—comic strip

313
get away—gifted

402
jackal—jaguar

443
loris—lovebird

445
lozenge—lunar

694
sew—shadow

695
shady—shamrock

792
tea—technetium

793
technic—telescope

How do you use the guide words? Guide words always appear in twos—one on the left and one on the right. The guide word on the left is the first dictionary entry on that page. The guide word on the right is the last word on the page.

Use the guide words on page 178 to help you answer the questions.

Choose the best answer.

1. The word *teenager* would follow which guide word?
   a. tea   c. technic
   b. technetium   d. telescope

Check your answer. Look at the third letter in each guide word and *teenager*. The letter *e* follows *c*. *Technetium* comes before *technic*. So the answer is **c**.

2. The word *combine* is most likely to appear on which page?
   a. 2   c. 313
   b. 142   d. 443

3. The word *lumpy* would be closest to which guide word?
   a. loris   c. lozenge
   b. lovebird   d. lunar

4. Which one of these words will not appear on page 2?
   a. aboard   c. above
   b. able   d. abbreviate

5. Which of these words will not appear on pages 694–695?
   a. several   c. shampoo
   b. sewing   d. shamble

6. You would find the word *yoga* on the page that has the guide words ___.
   a. yea and Yiddish   c. youthful and yummy
   b. yield and youth   d. yacht and yawl

What Makes a Riddle Funny

Question: How do you know when a gorilla is about to charge?
Answer: He takes out a credit card.

If you think this riddle is funny, you probably know that the word *charge* has two meanings. In the question it means to rush against. In the answer it means paying for something with a charge account. *Charge* is one of many words in the dictionary that has two or more meanings. All of these meanings are listed under the entry word.

Here are sample dictionary entries that show words with several meanings.

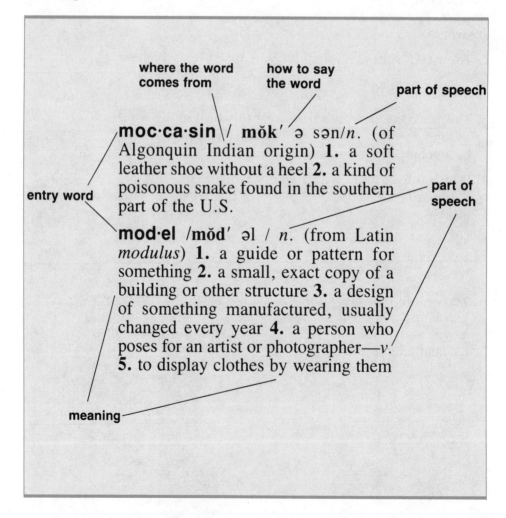

where the word comes from

how to say the word

part of speech

moc·ca·sin / mŏk′ ə sən/ *n.* (of Algonquin Indian origin) **1.** a soft leather shoe without a heel **2.** a kind of poisonous snake found in the southern part of the U.S.

entry word

part of speech

mod·el /mŏd′ əl / *n.* (from Latin *modulus*) **1.** a guide or pattern for something **2.** a small, exact copy of a building or other structure **3.** a design of something manufactured, usually changed every year **4.** a person who poses for an artist or photographer—*v.* **5.** to display clothes by wearing them

meaning

Look at the dictionary entries on page 180. Each entry word is in dark type. It is divided into syllables. Next, you see symbols. They tell you how to say the word. Then the dictionary tells you if the word is a noun (n) or a verb (v). Sometimes the dictionary also tells where a word came from. Finally, you see the meanings of the word. Each meaning has a number. Use the entries on page 180 to answer these questions.

Choose the best answer.

1. Which entry word has the same last syllable as *arson* / är´ sən /, and names two different things?
   a. moccasin
   b. model
   c. snake
   d. guide

Check your answer. The first entry word in dark type is divided into three parts. Its last syllable sounds the same as the last syllable in *arson*. It names a shoe or a snake. The answer is **a**.

2. The second syllable of *model* rhymes with which word?
   a. mode /mōd/
   b. bundle / bən-dəl /
   c. mall /mäl/
   d. bell /bĕl/

3. What is the number of the meaning of *model* used in this sentence: "Please model this coat at the fashion show"?
   a. 1
   b. 3
   c. 4
   d. 5

4. What kind of moccasin would you wear?
   a. an Indian
   b. a snake
   c. a shoe
   d. a heel

5. Which of these is not found in a dictionary entry?
   a. number of syllables
   b. how to say a word
   c. meaning
   d. jokes using the word

6. How are all entry words arranged in the dictionary?
   a. by number of syllables
   b. alphabetically
   c. by different meanings
   d. numerically

All About Snakes

It is a fact that snakes are deaf. Did you know that snakes never close their eyes? And snakes smell with their tongues as well as their noses. All snakes can swim. In fact, some snakes live in the water. These facts about snakes are from a book about snakes. How do you know what facts are in a book? A quick look at the table of contents at the front of a book will tell you what is in it.

The table of contents from the book on snakes is given below. It lists the chapters, or parts, of the book. How many chapters does this book have?

SNAKES

A table of contents is found in the front of a book. It follows the title page. It lists the chapters of the book in the order in which they appear.
   Use the table of contents on page 182 to answer these questions.

Choose the best answer.

1. The king snake eats other snakes for dinner. You will find more facts about what snakes eat in Chapter ___.
   a. 3   c. 9
   b. 1   d. 8

Check your answer. Facts about the food that snakes eat would be found in the chapter on eating habits. The answer is **d**.

2. How does a snake keep from getting too hot or too cold? You would most likely look in Chapter ___.
   a. 7   c. 2
   b. 11   d. 10

3. Some snakes, like the python, squeeze their enemies to death. What pages tell how other snakes protect themselves from the squeezers?
   a. 68–75   c. 32–47
   b. 12–17   d. 24–31

4. Three snakes in the U.S. are in danger of dying out. What chapter would list the names of these snakes?
   a. 9   c. 33
   b. 7   d. 11

5. People say that no snakes live in Ireland. On what page would you look to see if this is true?
   a. 48   c. 66
   b. 24   d. 18

6. What pages would tell how snakes are born?
   a. 48–51   c. 52–53
   b. 54–55   d. 24–31

The Sick Book

Ouch! You cut your finger. Why didn't all your blood run out? It would have if it were water. But there is something special in your blood. It makes the blood around your cut get thicker. And the blood gets so thick it forms a kind of plug where the cut is. This plug is called a clot. And it keeps your blood from running out.

This is only one of the handy facts from *The Sick Book* by Marie Winn. What else does this book talk about? The index at the back of the book will tell you. Some parts of this book's index are given below.

INDEX

accident, 88, 90
aches, 140
blood, 7–8, 18, 23–25,
    29–30, 35
    cells, 110–132
chicken pox, 43, 54–57
dust, 97, 99, 103
earache, 50, 140
germs, 8–16, 18, 20,
    24–26, 61–64, 66, 71,
    79, 98–94, 117
headache, 57, 59, 98
hearing, 136
    loss, 51
heart, 21, 30, 120–122, 130
injection, 68, 99, 102, 104
kidneys, 122
measles, 16, 43
    German, 59
mosquito bite, 82, 140

nausea, 70
pain, 8, 27–28, 32, 45, 140
poison, 13, 15, 120
    ivy, 96, 98
    sumac, 97
ragweed, 100, 102
rash, 96, 98
    chicken pox, 54–56
    measles, 97
shots. See injection
stitches, 27, 72
tetanus shot, 29
throat, 14–15, 34, 36,
    49–50, 64, 68
    hoarse, 46–47
    sore, 45, 64, 68
    strep, 45–46
travel sickness, 40–41
vitamins, 11
X-ray, 90–91

Entries in an index are listed alphabetically, from A to Z. Use the index from *The Sick Book* to answer these questions.

Choose the best answer.

1. If you want to know why you get sore throats, what pages in the book would you read?
   a. 45–46   c. 45, 64, 68
   b. 63, 65, 141   d. 12–14, 34

Check your answer. The key word is *throat*. There are three topics under the entry *throat*. The correct answer is **c**.

2. The words in the index are in alphabetical order. That means that *ragweed* comes before *rash* but right after __.
   a. poison ivy   c. pain
   b. chicken pox   d. poison sumac

3. Which page will tell all about the rash you get from the measles?
   a. 96   c. 54
   b. 97   d. 16

4. The pages that talk about poison ivy are __.
   a. 13, 15, 120   c. 97, 99
   b. 96, 98   d. 100, 102

5. To find out why you always feel sick in a car or bus, you would look on pages __.
   a. 50, 140   c. 70
   b. 40–41   d. 57, 59, 98

6. Which pages tell about shots?
   a. 88, 90, 91, 97   c. 68, 99, 102, 104
   b. 11, 29, 30, 32   d. 27, 72, 96, 98

Old Africa in South Carolina

The Yoruba African Kingdom has a king. The people are called Yorubas. They believe in an old African religion that has many gods. The Yoruba priests shave their heads. They believe in voodoo. But the Yoruba African Kingdom is not in Africa. It is in the forests of South Carolina—in the United States.

Where can you find facts about Africa and South Carolina? Take a trip to the library. You can read those facts and others in books kept there. Finding the book that you want is easy. You can do it with the help of the card catalog. Every library has one.

Study these examples of library catalog cards.

Author card: The first words tell the name of the person who wrote the book.

299.6
M
    Mbiti, John S.
       Introduction to African Religion

    New York, Praeger © 1975
    211 pp.

299.6
M
    AFRICA—RELIGION
    Mbiti, John S.
       Introduction to African Religion

    New York, Praeger © 1975
    211 pp.

Subject card: The first words tell what the book is about.

Title Card: The first words tell the name of the book.

299.6
M

    Introduction to African Religion
    John S. Mbiti

    New York, Praeger © 1975
    211 pp.

There are three kinds of catalog cards to help you find books. There are author cards, title cards, and subject cards. All three kinds of cards are in the card catalog in alphabetical order.

Choose the best answer.

1. You will find the author's card for the book *Introduction to African Religion* in the drawer marked ___.
  a. Ia–Ip
  b. Ja–Jo
  c. Ma–Mn
  d. Mo–Mz

Check your answer. The author cards are in alphabetical order beginning with the author's last name. The answer is **c**.

2. Suppose you only know the name of this book. You will find the title card in the drawer marked ___.
  a. Aa–Af
  b. Ia–Ip
  c. Ma–Mn
  d. Ra–Re

3. John S. Mbiti's book is about ___.
  a. religion
  b. African gods
  c. African religion
  d. old Africa

4. Which card will you use to look for other books about Africa?
  a. author card
  b. title card
  c. subject card
  d. any one of the three cards

5. Which card will you look at to find a book called *African Mask*?
  a. author card
  b. title card
  c. subject card
  d. any one of the three cards

6. Which cards will you look at to find any other books by John Mbiti?
  a. author cards
  b. title cards
  c. subject cards
  d. any one of the cards

How Hungry Is Your Anteater?

If someone asked you how long an anteater's tongue was, could you tell them it's more than one foot long? How would you find out that some tarantulas are shy and peaceful? Did you know that most antelopes live in Africa?

To find the facts, all you have to do is look in an encyclopedia. An encyclopedia is a set of books filled with facts about people, places, and things.

Each book in an encylopedia is called a volume. The articles in each book are listed in alphabetical order. So, once you know what topic you want information on, you can look it up. Use the encyclopedia volumes on the left to help answer these questions.

Choose the best answer.

1. Which volume would tell you which dinosaur's name, the brontosaurus or the stegosaurus, means *thunder lizard*?
   a. Volume 2
   b. Volume 5
   c. Volume 10
   d. Volume 11

   Check your answer. You are looking for information about dinosaurs. The answer is **a**.

2. A baby pig is called a farrow. Which volume would probably tell you if this was true or false?
   a. Volume 2
   b. Volume 5
   c. Volume 7
   d. Volume 8

3. Which volume would tell you about caps, gills, and other parts of a mushroom?
   a. Volume 2
   b. Volume 4
   c. Volume 6
   d. Volume 10

4. Which volume would tell you if a yak is an animal, a vegetable, or a new type of racing car?
   a. Volume 1
   b. Volume 9
   c. Volume 11
   d. Volume 12

5. You will probably never get caught in quicksand. But just to be sure, which volume will tell you where quicksand is found in the United States?
   a. Volume 1
   b. Volume 8
   c. Volume 10
   d. Volume 11

6. You want to know if the typewriter was invented before the sewing machine was. Which volumes would tell you?
   a. Volumes 10 and 11
   b. Volumes 6 and 11
   c. Volumes 10 and 12
   d. Volumes 4 and 12

New Facts, Anyone?

Anyone who loves trivia knows about the almanac. The almanac has lots of facts on all kinds of topics. It will tell you how many people live in Tulsa, Oklahoma. It will tell what time the sun will rise every day for the year. You can find out what Tom Seaver's ERA was in 1970. And it will tell you when Lynda (Wonder Woman) Carter's birthday is. It will even tell you how many hours of TV you probably watched last year.

A new almanac is written every year. The index of an almanac is often found in the front of the book. It lists all the topics in the almanac in alphabetical order. Parts of an almanac are given below.

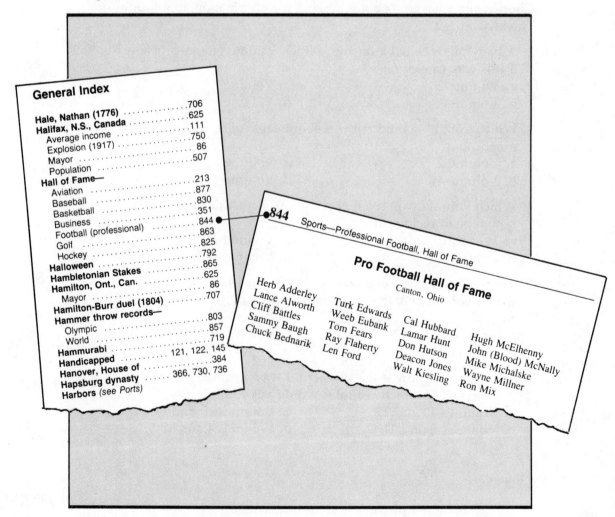

General Index

Hale, Nathan (1776) 706
Halifax, N.S., Canada 625
   Average income .111
   Explosion (1917) 750
   Mayor 86
   Population 507
Hall of Fame— 213
   Aviation 877
   Baseball 830
   Basketball 351
   Business 844
   Football (professional) 863
   Golf 825
   Hockey 792
Halloween 865
Hambletonian Stakes 625
Hamilton, Ont., Can. 86
   Mayor 707
Hamilton-Burr duel (1804)
Hammer throw records—
   Olympic 803
   World 857
Hammurabi 719
Handicapped 121, 122, 145
Hanover, House of 384
Hapsburg dynasty 366, 730, 736
Harbors (see Ports)

844   Sports—Professional Football, Hall of Fame

Pro Football Hall of Fame
Canton, Ohio

Herb Adderley
Lance Alworth
Cliff Battles
Sammy Baugh
Chuck Bednarik

Turk Edwards
Weeb Eubank
Tom Fears
Ray Flaherty
Len Ford

Cal Hubbard
Lamar Hunt
Don Hutson
Deacon Jones
Walt Kiesling

Hugh McElhenny
John (Blood) McNally
Mike Michalske
Wayne Millner
Ron Mix

An almanac is a reference book that has facts about many different topics. The index of the almanac lists all the topics in alphabetical order. Use the index on page 190 to answer these questions.

Choose the best answer.

1. On what page will you find facts about the 1917 explosion in Halifax, Nova Scotia?

    a. 625   c. 750

    b. 111   d. 507

Check your answer. The topic is Halifax. *Explosion* is listed under Halifax. So, the answer is **c**.

2. What page would tell who is in the Hockey Hall of Fame?

    a. 213   c. 825

    b. 863   d. 792

3. If you want to know what the world record for hammer throws is, what page would you look at?

    a. 803   c. 857

    b. 707   d. 719

4. How many pages in the almanac give the names of people in the Halls of Fame?

    a. 7   c. 1

    b. 0   d. 213

5. What is the date of the Alexander Hamilton-Aaron Burr duel?

    a. 1804   c. 1917

    b. 707   d. 1776

6. If you want information on harbors, you should __.

    a. turn to page 366   c. turn to *ports* in the index

    b. read the whole almanac   d. get another book

I Scream for Ice Cream

Did you know that over 47 million Americans scream for ice cream every day? Would you believe each American eats more than 17 pounds of ice cream each year? That's enough ice cream to fill the Grand Canyon!

Ice Cream has been around for ages. The Emperor Nero had it in Rome in the year 54 A.D. George Washington had ice cream in America in 1790. By 1875 the ice cream soda had been invented. And the ice cream sundae wasn't far behind. Then in 1904 the first ice cream cone was made.

Today you can choose from over 400 flavors of ice cream.

The facts in the story above did not come from the same source. Some facts came from an encyclopedia. Other facts were found in a book about fantastic facts. And some of the facts came from the almanac. The writer of this story used many sources.

Suppose you are writing a story based on facts. First, decide what facts you need. Then choose the sources where the facts are most likely to be found.

Choose the best answer.

1. Which of these sources would most likely tell what *xebec* means?
    a. an atlas
    c. a dictionary
    b. a science textbook
    d. an almanac

Check your answer. The source that gives meanings of words is the dictionary. The correct answer is **c**.

2. Where should you look to find the names of all the players in the Pro Football Hall of Fame?
    a. a newspaper
    c. a sports book
    b. an almanac
    d. an encyclopedia

3. Which of these will tell you how to make potato chips?
    a. a first aid book
    c. a dictionary
    b. an encyclopedia
    d. a cookbook

4. Where should you look to find out who invented the radio?
    a. an encyclopedia
    c. a newspaper
    b. a telephone book
    d. a science textbook

5. Where would you most likely find a map of the world?
    a. a newspaper
    c. a dictionary
    b. a book on gardens
    d. an encyclopedia

6. Which source would tell the score of yesterday's baseball game?
    a. an encyclopedia
    c. a newspaper
    b. a book on sports
    d. an almanac

Practice your reference skills as you follow the test tips on the next three pages. Put your answers on your answer sheet.

Test Tips: Most reference materials are arranged in alphabetical order. Study skills tests often include alphabetizing.

Choose the word that would come first if the four words or names were in alphabetical order.

1. a. atlas
   b. almanac
   c. average
   d. animal

2. a. mandolin
   b. mango
   c. manatee
   d. mantis

3. a. refreshment
   b. refuel
   c. refund
   d. reference

4. a. Gardner, Linda
   b. Gardner, Lewis
   c. Garfield, Larry
   d. Garrard, Lisa

Test Tips: Most study skills tests include questions about the purpose of each reference material. You should know where to look for certain kinds of facts.

Choose the best answer.

5. Which one of these alphabetically lists topics and the pages where the topics appear?
   a. index
   b. table of contents
   c. guide words
   d. dictionary entries

6. Which reference would tell you the different meanings of the word *stock*?
   a. almanac
   b. dictionary
   c. telephone book
   d. encyclopedia

7. Where would you find facts about Alexander Graham Bell, inventor of the telephone?
   a. dictionary
   b. almanac
   c. telephone book
   d. encyclopedia

8. Where would you look to find out Dave Righetti's pitching record last season?
   a. telephone book
   b. almanac
   c. dictionary
   d. a math book

Test Tips: Many tests include questions about a table of contents or an index. In this case, remember to read the questions first. Then find the correct answer on the index or table of contents. Here is the table of contents of the book on driving. Use it to answer the questions below.

Table of Contents

Choose the best answer.

1. Which chapter would most likely tell you that you need a license before you can drive?
   a. 1
   b. 2
   c. 3
   d. 4

2. You will probably find facts about early cars in the chapter that begins on page ___.
   a. 5
   b. 19
   c. 37
   d. 53

3. Buying a car is most likely to be a topic in chapter ___.
   a. 2
   b. 3
   c. 4
   d. 5

4. If you need to know how to fix a car's brakes, on what page would you begin looking?
   a. 19
   b. 37
   c. 53
   d. 71

TAKING TESTS

Here is the index of the same book on driving. Use it to answer the questions below.

Index

ads, car, 66	learner's permit, 22–23
auto accidents, 67–69	license, 19–25
buying, 53–59	maps, 72–73
camper, the first, 13	past, cars of the, 6–13
convertible, the first, 12	road test, 34–35
driver's manual, 24–25	safety, 74–75
engines, 60	tires, 46–47
insurance, 64–65	written test, 29–31

Choose the best answer.

1. To learn how to replace tires you must study pages ___.
   a. 67–69
   b. 46–47
   c. 60–61
   d. 12–13

2. You can find out about making a car safer on pages ___.
   a. 22–23
   b. 6–13
   c. 74–75
   d. 19–25

3. If you had to add the topic *road signs* to this index, where would you put it?
   a. after *road test*
   b. between *license* and *maps*
   c. after *cars of the past*
   d. at the bottom

4. If you're looking for a new car, which pages would be helpful to you?
   a. 53–59, 66
   b. 24–25, 66
   c. 72–73, 12
   d. 12, 13

5. On what pages are you most likely to find pictures of old cars?
   a. 53–59
   b. 6–13
   c. 22–23
   d. 24–25

6. Which pages describe the written test and the road test?
   a. 19–25, 22–23
   b. 64–65, 74–75
   c. 29–31, 34–35
   d. 24–25, 60

UNIT IV
TESTS

Test 1

Test 2

READING COMPREHENSION

Directions: This test will show how well you understand what you read. Read each passage. Then do the items that follow it. Choose the best answer for each item. On your answer sheet, fill in the space that goes with the answer you choose.

Which hand do you hold a pen with? Most people use their right hand. But one out of ten Americans uses the left hand. That is more than 20 million people all together.

No one is sure what makes a person right-handed or left-handed. Some people think that left-handed parents will have left-handed children. Children usually show which hand they will use by the age of six.

Long ago, left-handers were thought to be evil. The Romans believed that the right side of the body was the good side. They said the left side held evil spirits.

Most people don't really mind being left-handed these days. Yet left-handers still find it hard to use many items. Can openers, telephones, and watches are easier for right-handed people to use. So are cameras, guitars, and notebooks.

A few stores sell items made just for left-handers. The stores have special scissors, rulers, and tools. Now lefties do not feel "left out."

---

1. How many Americans are left-handed?
   a. about 10 million
   b. one out of 20
   c. about 20 million
   d. about 200 million

2. Long ago, left-handers were thought to be __.
   a. smart   c. loud
   b. shy   d. evil

3. Items for left-handers are now __.
   a. only for children
   b. only for parents
   c. easier to get
   d. harder to get

4. Watches are made for right-handers because __.
   a. most people are left-handed
   b. most people are right-handed
   c. left-handers don't wear watches
   d. left-handers can't tell time

5. Which of these is the best title for this passage?
   a. "The Facts About Lefties"
   b. "Left-Handers in Rome"
   c. "Stores for Left-Handers"
   d. "Famous Left-Handers"

A special group of people live in a rain forest in the Philippines. The people are called the Tasaday, or the People of the Caves. The Tasaday still live the way people did long ago. They use stone tools. They make fire by rubbing two sticks together. Their clothes are made from leaves.

The Tasaday do not have to hunt or farm. They find food easily in the forest and streams. Only a few hours are needed to get food for the whole group. Men and women share all the work. There is no leader.

The Tasaday spend time together after gathering their food. They talk, play, and swim. The children are kind and peaceful and never need to be punished. The Tasaday language has no words for war or anger.

No one knew about the Tasaday until 1967. That year, a man from another tribe happened to find them. Until then, the Tasaday had been hidden for about 2,000 years.

Now, 55,000 acres of land are set aside for the Tasaday. Lumber companies wanted to cut down the forest, but now they cannot. No one may enter the forest without permission. So far this has helped the Tasaday continue to live the kind of life they are used to.

---

6. The homes of the Tasaday are probably __.
  a. trees   c. cabins
  b. caves   d. houses

7. How do the Tasaday make fire?
  a. by striking a match
  b. by using a lighter
  c. by rubbing sticks together
  d. by waiting for lightning

8. The Tasaday probably have no word for war because __.
  a. they never have wars
  b. all their words have six letters
  c. they cannot say the "w" sound
  d. they never speak

9. Why do you think land was set aside for the Tasaday?
  a. to teach them how to farm
  b. to punish them for hiding
  c. to help protect their way of life
  d. to build a lumber company

10. This story is mostly about __.
  a. clothes made of leaves
  b. the Philippine rain forest
  c. lumber companies
  d. people called the Tasaday

The Bat

By day the bat is cousin to the mouse.
He likes the attic of an aging house.

His fingers make a hat about his head.
His pulse beat is so slow we think him dead.

He loops in crazy figures half the night
Among the trees that face the corner light.

But when he brushes up against a screen,
We are afraid of what our eyes have seen.

For something is amiss or out of place
When mice with wings can wear a human face.

Theodore Roethke

---

11. Where does the bat live by day?
a. in an attic
b. in a tree
c. in a corner
d. on a screen

12. What is the hat around the bat's head?
a. its hair
b. its cap
c. its wings
d. its hands

13. By day, the bat probably stays ___.
a. in the air
b. very still
c. in a tree
d. on the roof

14. The poet is afraid when the bat ___.
a. flies down from a tree
b. sleeps in the attic
c. brushes up against a screen
d. wears a hat

15. What does the poet think about the bat's face?
a. It looks old.
b. It looks dark.
c. It looks crazy.
d. It looks human.

Many people will never forget the night of October 30, 1938. Millions of Americans were sitting at home, listening to the radio. What they heard caused quite a scare.

The Mercury Theater was doing its weekly radio show. The show that night was based on a book called *War of the Worlds* by H.G. Wells. The book tells how Martians land on Earth and kill all the people.

Orson Welles was head of the show. He wanted to make the story seem real. He decided to do the story as a news program.

The show began with music and weather reports. Soon the music was stopped by special news bulletins. First the reports said something had blown up on the planet Mars. Later they said a large spaceship had landed in New Jersey. Finally the reports said Martians were killing everyone with ray guns and poison gas.

People listening to their radios got very scared. Many of them did not realize the show was a joke. The police got thousands of calls from worried people all over the U.S. Some people ran around wildly in the streets. Others got in cars and headed west.

The show had been a giant Halloween joke that worked too well. The show also taught an important lesson. Some people are willing to believe any news they hear on the radio—if it sounds real.

16. Orson Welles was __ .
   a. a Martian
   b. a book writer
   c. head of a radio show
   d. a police officer

17. The news reports said that Martians had landed __ .
   a. in New York
   b. in New Jersey
   c. on Mars
   d. outside America

18. People believed the news because __ .
   a. the show sounded real
   b. people believed in Martians
   c. newspapers wrote about it
   d. police said it was true

19. People got scared because __ .
   a. their radios didn't work
   b. they thought they would die
   c. they saw Martians
   d. their cars wouldn't start

20. This story is mostly about __ .
   a. the state of New Jersey
   b. the life of Orson Welles
   c. music and weather
   d. a scary radio show

VOCABULARY

Directions. This test will show if you can recognize words that have the same meaning, words that have opposite meanings, words that sound alike, and words that have several meanings.

For items 1–8, choose the word or phrase that means the same, or almost the same, as the word in dark type. Mark your answers on your answer sheet.

1. **unfastens** the lock
   a. turns
   b. closes
   c. changes
   d. opens

2. the building **collapsed**
   a. was built
   b. was opened
   c. fell
   d. burned

3. **handle** difficult problems
   a. have
   b. deal with
   c. hold
   d. be upset by

4. an **unpleasant** person
   a. not pretty
   b. not happy
   c. not nice
   d. not pleased

5. **intended** to leave early
   a. planned
   b. tried
   c. departed
   d. believed

6. an **anxious** feeling
   a. good
   b. nervous
   c. funny
   d. lonely

7. **vary** greatly
   a. work
   b. look
   c. be different
   d. feel

8. a **stationary** object
   a. fast
   b. paper
   c. not moving
   d. not stopping

For items 9–16, choose the word or phrase that means the opposite of the word in dark type.

9. remained **motionless**
   a. still
   b. moving
   c. alone
   d. without feelings

10. **conceal** a letter
    a. hide
    b. seal up
    c. write
    d. reveal

11. a **fiction** story
    a. made up
    b. boring
    c. exciting
    d. true

12. a **talkative** child
    a. brilliant
    b. quiet
    c. small
    d. young

13. a **just** decision
    a. unfair
    b. right
    c. quick
    d. one and only

14. **neglected** his family
    a. remembered
    b. forgot
    c. raised
    d. left

15. the earth's **surface**
    a. flatness
    b. inside
    c. outside
    d. bigness

16. an **initial** thought
    a. smart
    b. last
    c. stupid
    d. first

For items 17–22, choose the sentence in which the word in dark type means the same as the definition given.

17. one and only
   a. Not a **soul** came to her party.
   b. Helen was the **sole** person there.
   c. We believed his **soul** went to heaven.

18. important
   a. The **major** gave out orders.
   b. Snow created **major** problems for drivers.
   c. My cousin is an English **major** in college.

19. make a painful sound
   a. Bill has **grown** six inches this year.
   b. Some people **groan** when their shoulders hurt.
   c. The pain has **grown** worse.

20. threw
   a. Barbara **cast** the stone 50 yards.
   b. Juanita was **cast** in the role of Juliet.
   c. For whom did you **cast** your vote?

21. test
   a. Sam took a **trial** run on the race course.
   b. The man went on **trial**.
   c. The murder **trial** lasted ten weeks.

22. new or different
   a. Alicia wrote her first **novel**.
   b. She had a **novel** idea for a story.
   c. I have read every **novel** by Mark Twain.

STUDY SKILLS

Directions: This test will show how well you can get and use information from maps, tables, graphs, and reference materials.

Read each question. Four answers are given, but only one is right. On your answer sheet, fill in the answer space for the best answer.

ARRIVALS			
Flight	From	Gate	Time
AA 124	Detroit	1	6:30 a.m.
TW 193	Newark	10	7:00 a.m.
UA 701	Cleveland	5	7:15 a.m.
EA 195	Washington, DC	2	11:00 a.m.
DL 707	Miami	9	11:15 a.m.

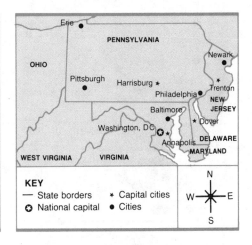

KEY
— State borders   ★ Capital cities
✪ National capital   ● Cities

1. Where would you be most likely to find this table?
   a. school   c. airport
   b. store   d. zoo

2. When does flight DL 707 arrive?
   a. 7:00 a.m.   c. 11:00 a.m.
   b. 7:15 a.m.   d. 11:15 a.m.

3. At which gate can you meet someone on the plane from Newark?
   a. 10   c. 5
   b. 9   d. 2

4. Where does flight UA 701 come from?
   a. Detroit   c. Miami
   b. Cleveland   d. Newark

5. What is the capital city of Pennsylvania?
   a. Annapolis   c. Harrisburg
   b. Pittsburgh d. Philadelphia

6. Erie is located ___ of Pittsburgh.
   a. north   c. east
   b. south   d. west

7. Which state borders Pennsylvania on the west?
   a. New Jersey c. Delaware
   b. Ohio   d. Virginia

8. Our national capital is very near to ___, the capital city of Maryland.
   a. Dover   c. Annapolis
   b. Washington d. Baltimore

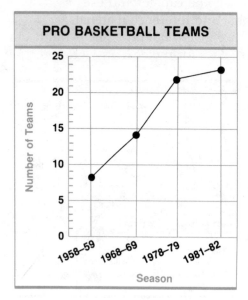

PRO BASKETBALL TEAMS

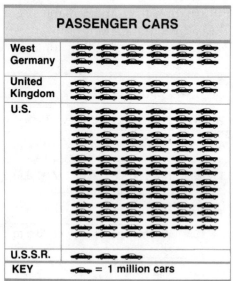

PASSENGER CARS

9. This visual material is a __.
   a. line graph
   b. bar graph
   c. pie graph
   d. pictograph

10. The graph shows that the number of teams has gone __.
    a. steadily down
    b. steadily up
    c. flat
    d. down and up

11. How many teams played during the 1968–1969 season?
    a. 16   c. 14
    b. 15   d. 10

12. How many more teams played in 1981–82 than in 1978–79?
    a. 23   c. 1
    b. 22   d. 0

13. This graph shows that there are the most cars in __.
    a. United Kingdom   c. U.S.S.R.
    b. West Germany   d. U.S.

14. How many cars are there in the U.S.S.R.?
    a. 30
    b. 3 million
    c. 3
    d. 300

15. Which country ranks second in number of cars?
    a. United Kingdom c. U.S.
    b. West Germany   d. U.S.S.R.

16. How many more cars are there in West Germany than in the United Kingdom?
    a. 4 million   c. 4
    b. 19 million   d. 19

Directions: Use this table of contents to answer the questions below.

Recreation Guide

Contents

17. Which topic might tell about places that rent canoes?
    a. Beaches   c. Boating
    b. Camping   d. Skating

18. On which page would you begin reading about places along the shores?
    a. 5   c. 11
    b. 7   d. 15

19. On which page would you begin reading about winter sports?
    a. 15   c. 27
    b. 19   d. 30

Directions: Answer the questions below about how and where to get information.

20. Which one of these is not arranged alphabetically?
    a. index
    b. encyclopedia
    c. table of contents
    d. dictionary

21. Which is the best source for yesterday's football scores?
    a. newspaper   c. dictionary
    b. map   d. encyclopedia

22. For which of these would you use a dictionary?
    a. to find China's neighbors
    b. to learn how the Chinese live
    c. to find out the latest news from China
    d. to learn how to say *Mandarin*

23. Which would best show the directions from New York City to Toronto?
    a. a road map
    b. a book on cities
    c. an almanac
    d. a newspaper

24. Which would be the best source for finding information on the life of Paul Revere?
    a. almanac
    b. news magazine
    c. encyclopedia
    d. book on the U.S.

READING COMPREHENSION

Directions: This test offers several reading selections. After each selection there are some exercises. Read each selection and then answer the questions. Four answers are given for each exercise, but only one of these answers is right. On your answer sheet, fill in the space that goes with the answer you choose.

You may have the same shoe size as someone else. You may also have the same color eyes or hair. But there is one thing that can't be the same. That is your fingerprints.

No two fingerprints are alike. The curving lines on each finger make a pattern. Each print never changes, except to get bigger as you grow.

What good are fingerprints? First, they help us to hold things. You know how the lines on a tire help it grip the road. Fingerprints help us grip things the same way.

Fingerprints also help police identify people. Police look for fingerprints where a crime has taken place. Dust is used to show the fingerprints. It can show prints on metal, wood, or even paper.

Before 1903, police did not use fingerprints. They identified people only by their pictures and body size. Then a strange thing happened. Police found two prisoners in Kansas. One was named Will West. The other was named William West. Both men looked the same. The only way to tell them apart was by checking their fingerprints.

---

1. Fingerprints are made up of ___.
   a. straight lines
   b. curving lines
   c. pointed lines
   d. lines and dots

2. Fingerprints never change except to get ___.
   a. darker   c. bigger
   b. lighter   d. smaller

3. Without fingerprints, we might find it harder to ___.
   a. hold things
   b. drop things
   c. lift things
   d. forget things

4. If police did not check fingerprints, they might ___.
   a. take more pictures
   b. find more prisoners
   c. get people mixed up
   d. use special dust

5. What is the main idea of this selection?
   a. where crimes take place
   b. how police work
   c. how fingerprints change
   d. how fingerprints are used

[1]Many kinds of birds have disappeared from the earth forever. The dodo bird is one famous example. Dodo birds once lived on an island in the Indian Ocean. They were large, gentle birds that couldn't fly or swim.

[2]In the early 1600's, the first explorers came to the island. They killed many of the dodo birds and used them for food or bait. Others died of diseases. The last dodo on earth is supposed to have died in 1681.

[3]The Atlantic puffin is another bird that has seemed to be in danger. The puffin is like a dodo in some ways. It has a large body and tiny wings. Many puffins once lived on Egg Rock Island, Maine. But hunters killed too many of them. The puffins disappeared from the island.

[4]For eight years, scientists tried to get puffins to return to the island. Finally, they were successful. The scientists made wooden models of the puffins and placed them all around the island. In the summer of 1981, the puffins returned.

---

6. The first paragraph of this story is mostly about __.
   a. the changing earth
   b. dodo birds
   c. early explorers
   d. fishing in the Indian Ocean

7. We will never see another dodo bird because __.
   a. they are afraid of people
   b. they live on a secret island
   c. explorers took them away
   d. the last one died in 1681

8. What is the main idea of paragraph 3?
   a. Puffins were in danger.
   b. A puffin has tiny wings.
   c. Puffins lived in Maine.
   d. Explorers killed puffins.

9. Why are scientists working on puffins?
   a. to learn how to catch them
   b. to teach them to fly
   c. to save them from dying out
   d. to show them how to swim

10. Puffins must like to be where there are __.
   a. explorers
   b. other puffins
   c. wooden ships
   d. dodo birds

On her 16th birthday, Mary Cassatt told her father she wanted to be a painter. "I would almost rather see you dead" was his answer.

In the middle 1800's, the artist's world was a man's world. Most young women could not think of becoming a painter. Women were expected to marry and raise a family. But Mary had always tried to think for herself. She tried hard to change her father's mind. Finally, he agreed that she could study painting in Paris, France.

She went to Paris at the age of 22 and set to work on her painting. Slowly, other artists began to hear about her work. She painted the pictures that would make her famous. They were pictures of children and of mothers caring for their children.

When she was nearly 50, Mary showed 100 of her paintings at an art show in Paris. Her paintings were the only ones in the show. They were a great success.

The greatest praise of all came from Mary's father. Much had changed since Mary had told her father she wanted to be a painter. She had become one of the best painters in the world.

---

11. This selection is mostly about Mary Cassatt's ___.
   a. birthday paty
   b. trip to Paris
   c. life as a painter
   d. art show in Paris

12. Mary must have lived in Paris ___.
   a. for a year
   b. since she was 16
   c. until she was 22
   d. for more than 25 years

13. What pictures made Mary Cassatt famous?
   a. pictures of children
   b. pictures of animals
   c. pictures of buildings
   d. pictures of her father

14. At the end of the story, Mary's father must have been ___.
   a. angry
   b. sick
   c. proud
   d. lost

15. Where would you expect to find Mary Cassatt's work?
   a. in a shopping center
   b. in an art museum
   c. in a post office
   d. in a science museum

The Fog

Slowly, the fog,
Hunch-shouldered with a gray face,
Arms wide, advances,
Finger-tips touching the way
Past the dark houses
And dark gardens of roses.
Up the short street from the harbor,
Slowly the fog,
Seeking, seeking;
Arms wide, shoulders hunched,
Searching, searching.
Out through the streets to the fields,
Slowly, the fog—
A blind man hunting the moon.

F.R. McCreary

---

16. In this poem, the fog seems to be a __.
a. gray animal
b. person
c. flower
d. ship

17. The poem shows how the fog __.
a. spreads out over the town
b. comes into a house
c. gets behind the moon
d. smells the flowers

18. When is the fog moving?
a. in the morning
b. on a Sunday
c. at noon
d. at night

19. What does the poet say the fog is looking for?
a. the roses
b. the harbor
c. the moon
d. the sun

20. What is the last place the fog went to?
a. the street
b. the fields
c. the houses
d. the harbor

VOCABULARY

Directions. This test will show how well you understand the meaning of different words and if you recognize words and phrases that have the same meaning.

For items 1–8 choose the word or phrase that means the same, or almost the same, as the word in dark type. Mark your answers on your answer sheet.

1. **pursued** a robber
   a. met
   b. stopped
   c. chased
   d. caught

2. **approaching** a town
   a. leaving
   b. coming toward
   c. seeing
   d. living in

3. **connect** two wires
   a. unwind
   b. separate
   c. join
   d. send

4. have **surgery** done
   a. an operation
   b. work
   c. magic
   d. building

5. **established** a record
   a. listened to
   b. bought
   c. set
   d. tabled

6. **gulped** his food
   a. cooked
   b. served
   c. bought
   d. swallowed

7. a **suspense** movie
   a. long
   b. mystery
   c. funny
   d. superior

8. **commonplace** objects
   a. complex
   b. strange
   c. ordinary
   d. motionless

For items 9–16 read each sentence beginning. Choose the word or phrase that best completes each sentence.

9. A negative effect is ___.
   a. helpful
   b. harmful
   c. important
   d. not important

10. A town that is distant is not ___.
   a. crowded
   b. large
   c. near
   d. far away

11. When you rotate something you ___.
   a. stop it
   b. turn it
   c. buy it
   d. hide it

12. An examination is a ___.
   a. tall building
   b. large country
   c. terrible event
   d. test

13. If you are out of work temporarily, you are out ___.
   a. for a short time
   b. for a long time
   c. for a year
   d. for several years

14. An offender is someone who ___.
   a. is unhappy
   b. runs fast
   c. breaks the law
   d. is very nervous

15. If you do something repeatedly, you do it ___.
   a. one time
   b. quickly
   c. over and over
   d. slowly

16. If something is unnoticed, it is ___.
   a. not seen
   b. huge
   c. unusual
   d. underwater

For items 17–22 read the selection below. Notice the words in dark type. Choose the word or phrase that best answers each question about the words in dark type.

On January 15, 1919, an unusual **disaster** happened in Boston. This tragedy occurred when an **immense** storage tank broke open and spilled two-and-a-half million gallons of molasses in the street. After the huge tank **shattered**, a river of molasses rolled along the street and drowned everything in its way. Molasses is usually thought of as being slow, but this river moved very **rapidly**. Most of the **victims**, people hurt or killed, were trapped without warning. Some people **attempted** to swim in the sticky river, but their tries soon failed. In all, 21 people were killed in the "Great Molasses Flood."

---

17. What does **disaster** mean in the selection?
a. event   c. tragedy
b. river   d. day

18. What does **immense** mean in the selection?
a. immediate   c. wooden
b. molasses   d. huge

19. What does **shattered** mean in the selection?
a. became empty   c. swam
b. was filled up d. broke

20. What does **rapidly** mean in the selection?
a. slowly   c. sticky
b. quickly   d. stupidly

21. What does **victims** mean in the selection?
a. people   c. swimmers
b. people hurt   d. watchers

22. What does **attempted** mean in the selection?
a. wanted   c. failed
b. swam   d. tried

STUDY SKILLS

Directions: This test will show how well you can get and use information from maps, tables, graphs, and reference materials.

Read each question. Four answers are given, but only one is right. On your answer sheet, fill in the answer space for the best answer.

CLIMATE IN SOME CITIES		
City	January	July
Boise, Idaho	32°F	75°F
Cheyenne, Wyoming	27°F	69°F
Denver, Colorado	30°F	73°F
Great Falls, Montana	27°F	69°F
Reno, Nevada	32°F	69°F
Salt Lake City, Utah	28°F	77°F
Source: Statistical Abstract of U.S. 1978		

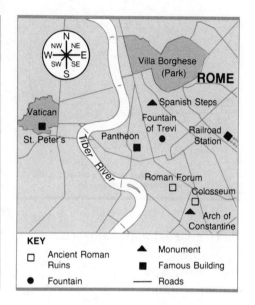

KEY
☐ Ancient Roman Ruins
▲ Monument
■ Famous Building
● Fountain
— Roads

1. The above table shows the average daily __ in some Rocky Mountain cities during winter and summer.
   a. temperature
   b. rainfall
   c. weather
   d. sunshine

2. Which city is the hottest in July?
   a. Boise
   b. Denver
   c. Reno
   d. Salt Lake City

3. The two cities that have the same average daily temperature in January are Boise and __.
   a. Denver
   b. Reno
   c. Cheyenne
   d. Great Falls

4. The above map tells you that the Pantheon is a __.
   a. famous building
   b. road
   c. fountain
   d. monument

5. The Vatican is __ of the Tiber River.
   a. north
   b. south
   c. east
   d. west

6. From the railroad station to the Spanish Steps, you must travel __.
   a. SE
   b. NE
   c. SW
   d. NW

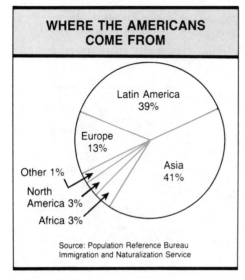

WHERE THE AMERICANS COME FROM

Latin America 39%

Europe 13%

Other 1%

North America 3%

Africa 3%

Asia 41%

Source: Population Reference Bureau
Immigration and Naturalization Service

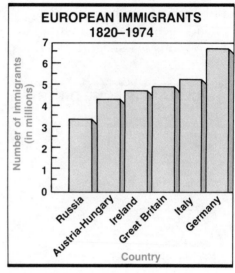

EUROPEAN IMMIGRANTS 1820–1974

Number of Immigrants (in millions)

Russia
Austria-Hungary
Ireland
Great Britain
Italy
Germany

Country

7. This visual material is a __.
   a. line graph
   b. bar graph
   c. pie graph
   d. pictograph

8. The graph shows that more new Americans come from __ than any other part of the world.
   a. Asia   c. Africa
   b. Europe   d. Latin America

9. For every 100 new Americans, how many come from Africa?
   a. 1   c. 3
   b. 2   d. 13

10. How many more Latin Americans come to the U.S. than Europeans?
    a. 26%   c. 39%
    b. 29%   d. 13%

11. This graph shows that most of the Europeans that came to the U.S. were from __.
    a. Russia   c. Italy
    b. Austria   d. Germany

12. From which of the six countries did the smallest number of immigrants come?
    a. Russia   c. Ireland
    b. Austria   d. Germany

13. How many more immigrants came from Germany than from Ireland?
    a. 2   c. 2,000
    b. 200   d. 2,000,000

14. Which country ranks second if Germany ranks first?
    a. Austria-Hungary
    b. Great Britain
    c. Italy
    d. Ireland

216

Directions: Below is a set of volumes of an encyclopedia. Use this set of volumes to answer these questions.

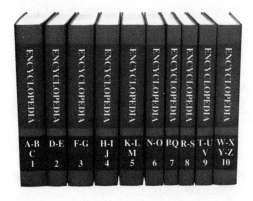

15. Which volume would you choose to read about Mercator, the mapmaker?
    a. Volume 1   c. Volume 5
    b. Volume 3   d. Volume 7

16. In which volume would you find pictures of Mars, Venus, Earth, and all the planets?
    a. Volume 5   c. Volume 1
    b. Volume 7   d. Volume 9

17. Which volume would tell about the art, history, music, and way of life in India?
    a. Volume 2   c. Volume 6
    b. Volume 4   d. Volume 8

Directions: Answer the questions below about how and where to get information.

18. Which would best show the country on the north border of Mexico?
    a. a calendar
    b. a newspaper
    c. a dictionary
    d. a map

19. In which of these would you most easily find how to say the word *zoophyte*?
    a. a map of the zoo
    b. a language book
    c. a dictionary
    d. a newspaper

20. For which of these would you use an almanac?
    a. to learn the meaning of *sports*
    b. to find out how sports began
    c. to learn the latest sports records
    d. to find out who plays the Lakers tomorrow

21. The index in the almanac is arranged —.
    a. by the order of the alphabet
    b. by date
    c. by number
    d. by the order of importance

Vocabulary Glossary

Here are all the new words you learned in the vocabulary lessons and their meanings. Remember, sometimes a word can have more than one meaning. The meanings listed here fit the way the words were used in the stories.

accurate—correct
achieved—did something very good
admitted—confessed
adventurous—exciting or daring
advertised—offered for sale in ads
aid—help
ambitions—strong hopes or goals
annoy—bother or disturb
anxious—worried or nervous
approaching—coming near
approximately—nearly reaching an amount
assist—help
assistant—helper
athlete—sports player
autobiography—story of a person's life written by the person

blend—mix
bogged—stuck

capture—take or catch by force
case—problem brought to court
cast—put in or throw
cavern—underground cave
cavity—hole
cheap—costing very little
climate—weather conditions
coat—layer or covering
collapsed—fell
collided—ran into or crashed

comedians—people who tell jokes
common—usual or normal
commonplace—ordinary
complex—hard to understand
composition—mixture of materials
conceal—hide
confirm—check on
connect—join together
consume—use up or eat
conversed—talked

deed—an act someone did
demonstrate—explain by showing examples
departed—left
destination—ending point
devices—inventions
disbelief—a feeling of not trusting
disconnect—separate
distant—faraway
dough—mixture to be baked
drought—time of little rain

elected—voted into office
emerge—come out
employees—hired workers
encountered—met with something by surprise
errorless—correct or without a mistake
established—set or set up
estimate—judge or guess
examination—test

218

examine—study or test

fashion—way of doing things
fiction—made-up stories
finish—a final covering
flee—run away or escape

grate—chop up
groan—make a sad or painful
 sound
gulped—swallowed

hale—healthy
handle—deal with
heed—pay attention to
herd—group of animals
humorous—funny or amusing

illuminated—lit up
immense—huge
inclined—leaning or slanted
indestructible—not able to be
 destroyed
initial—first
inquired—asked
inspected—studied or looked at
instance—case or example
intended—planned

just—fair or right

knead—mix by pushing together

lapse—pause
lessen—make less or easier
lifelike—like real life
limited—cut short

magnifies—makes larger
major—important
maximum—top or highest
motionless—still or not moving

negative—bad or harmful

neglected—forgot to do something
novel—fiction book; new or
 different

offender—someone who breaks
 the law
office—job or position

participate—take part or join
peacefulness—peacetime or calm
performances—acts or shows
perilous—likely to lead to danger
permit—let or allow
physical—about the body
platform—ideas you speak out for
popular—well-liked
positive—good or helpful
praise—say something is good
precisely—exactly
predictions—forecasts
proceeded—went on or continued
pursued—chased after

questioning—asking questions

repeatedly—over and over
resides—lives
rotate—turn around or spin
run—be in an election

scraping—dragging
secure—keep in place
sense—good thinking
sentences—judgments or
 decisions
series—group of related things
serve—do work for
shudder—shake from fear
sole—one and only
species—a kind of plant or animal
speechless—not able to talk
stationary—still or not moving

steal—take illegally
store—keep somewhere
stride—a walking step
submerge—sink
substitute—take the place of
sufficient—enough
supports—holds up
surface—outside of an object
surgery—an operation
survive—stay alive
suspense—a feeling of mystery
swiftness—quickness or speed

talkative—noisy
temporarily—for a short time
tension—feeling of nervousness
term—set period of time
tragedy—terrible event
transfer—shift or move
transform—change
trial—court case or test

triumphed—gained victory or won

unexpected—not hoped for
unfastens—opens or unlocks
unharmed—not hurt
unnoticed—not seen
unopened—closed
unpleasant—not nice
unsuspecting—trusting or
    believing

vanished—disappeared
vary—change or be different
vehicles—things people ride in
vessel—ship
view—opinion or belief

wholly—totally or completely
wondrous—surprising or amazing
worldwide—all over the world

youngster—child

Answer Key

UNIT I READING COMPREHENSION

Pages 8–9: 1. b, 2. a, 3. c, 4. b, 5. c
Pages 10–11: 1. a, 2. b, 3. b, 4. c, 5. a
Pages 12–13: 1. c, 2. a, 3. b, 4. a, 5. c
Pages 14–15: 1. b, 2. c, 3. a, 4. c, 5. b, 6. c
Pages 16–17: 1. c, 2. b, 3. a, 4. b, 5. c, 6. b
Pages 18–19: 1. b, 2. c, 3. c, 4. a, 5. b, 6. a
Pages 20–21: 1. c, 2. a, 3. b, 4. c, 5. b, 6. a
Pages 22–23: 1. a, 2. b, 3. b, 4. a, 5. c, 6. c
Page 24: 1. d, 2. b, 3. c, 4. a, 5. b
Page 25: 1. b, 2. c, 3. c, 4. a, 5. d
Page 26: 1. c, 2. b, 3. d, 4. a, 5. b
Page 27: 1. b, 2. c, 3. b, 4. a, 5. d
Pages 28–29: 1. a, 2. c, 3. b, 4. b, 5. c
Pages 30–31: 1. c, 2. a, 3. b, 4. c, 5. b
Pages 32–33: 1. c, 2. a, 3. b, 4. c, 5. b
Pages 34–35: 1. a, 2. c, 3. b, 4. b, 5. a, 6. c
Pages 36–37: 1. b, 2. a, 3. b, 4. c, 5. c, 6. b
Pages 38–39: 1. b, 2. c, 3. a, 4. b, 5. c, 6. a
Pages 40–41: 1. b, 2. c, 3. a, 4. c, 5. b, 6. c
Pages 42–43: 1. c, 2. b, 3. a, 4. b, 5. c 6. c
Pages 44–45: 1. a, 2. c, 3. b, 4. a, 5. c, 6. a
Page 46: 1. b, 2. a, 3. d, 4. d, 5. c
Page 47: 1. b, 2. a, 3. d, 4. c, 5. d
Page 48: 1. c, 2. b, 3. b, 4. d, 5. a
Page 49: 1. a, 2. b, 3. a, 4. c, 5. d
Pages 50–51: 1. c, 2. b, 3. a, 4. c, 5. b
Pages 52–53: 1. b, 2. c, 3. a, 4. c, 5. b
Pages 54–55: 1. c, 2. b, 3. a, 4. b, 5. c
Pages 56–57: 1. c, 2. b, 3. c, 4. a, 5. b, 6. a
Pages 58–59: 1. b, 2. a, 3. b, 4. c, 5. a, 6. b
Pages 60–61: 1. b, 2. b, 3. c, 4. a, 5. b, 6. c
Pages 62–63: 1. b, 2. c, 3. b, 4. a, 5. c, 6. b
Pages 64–65: 1. c, 2. b, 3. a, 4. c, 5. b, 6. a
Pages 66–67: 1. a, 2. c, 3. a, 4. b, 5. c, 6. c
Pages 68–69: 1. a, 2. c, 3. c, 4. b, 5. c, 6. b
Pages 70–71: 1. b, 2. c, 3. c, 4. a, 5. c, 6. b
Pages 72–73: 1. a, 2. b, 3. c, 4. a, 5. c, 6. c
Pages 74–75: 1. b, 2. a, 3. b, 4. c, 5. c, 6. b
Page 76: 1. d, 2. b, 3. b, 4. c
Page 77: 1. c, 2. b, 3. a, 4. c, 5. d
Page 78: 1. c, 2. d, 3. b, 4. b

UNIT II VOCABULARY

Pages 84–85: A. 1. intended, 2. encountered, 3. maximum, 4. adventurous, 5. neglected, 6. collided, 7. demonstrate, 8. achieved; B. 1. b, 2. a, 3. b, 4. c

Pages 86–87: A. 1. climate, 2. positive, 3. annoy, 4. capture, 5. negative, 6. species, 7. survive, 8. consume; B. 1. b, 2. c, 3. a, 4. c

Pages 88–89: A. 1. flee, 2. proceeded, 3. swiftness, 4. estimate, 5. pursued, 6. employees, 7. approximately, 8. offender; B. 1. b, 2. c, 3. a, 4. b

Pages 90–91: A. 1. participate, 2. transfer, 3. ambitions, 4. triumphed, 5. rotate, 6. series, 7. athlete, 8. stride; B. 1. b, 2. c, 3. b, 4. a

Pages 92–93: A. 1. suspense, 2. heed, 3. humorous, 4. shudder, 5. anxious, 6. tension, 7. popular, 8. perilous; B. 1. b, 2. a, 3. c, 4. b

Pages 96–97: A. 1. approaching, 2. distant, 3. complex, 4. permit, 5. illuminated, 6. magnifies, 7. limited, 8. assist; B. 1. c, 2. b, 3. a, 4. b

Pages 98–99: A. 1. unexpected, 2. unopened, 3. disbelief, 4. unnoticed, 5. unpleasant, 6. accurate, 7. initial, 8. major; B. 1. a, 2. b, 3. a, 4. c

Pages 100–101: A. 1. assistant, 2. precisely, 3. disconnect, 4. unsuspecting, 5. unharmed, 6. unfastens, 7. common, 8. conceal; B. 1. b, 2. c, 3. a, 4. c

Pages 104–105: A. 1. lessen, 2. sense, 3. dough, 4. praise, 5. grate, 6. groan, 7. cheap, 8. knead; B. 1. b, 2. b, 3. a, 4. b

Pages 106–107: A. 1. stationary, 2. hale, 3. aid, 4. steal, 5. vary, 6. herd, 7. wholly, 8. lapse; B. 1. a, 2. a, 3. b, 4. a

Page 108: 1. b, 2. a, 3. c, 4. a, 5. b, 6. a, 7. d, 8. d

Page 109: 1. c, 2, c, 3. a, 4. d, 5. b, 6. c, 7. b, 8. c

Page 110: 1. b, 2. c, 3. a, 4. c, 5. c, 6. d, 7. a, 8. b

Page 111: 1. a, 2. c, 3. a, 4. a, 5. b, 6. b

Pages 116–117: A. 1. a, 2. c, 3. b, 4. c, 5. a, 6. c, 7. b, 8. a

Pages 118–119: A. 1. b, 2. b, 3. a, 4. b, 5. a, 6. a, 7. c, 8. c

Pages 120–121: A. 1. c, 2. b, 3. a, 4. c, 5. b, 6. c, 7. c, 8. c

Pages 122–123: A. 1. a, 2. c, 3. b, 4. c, 5. a, 6. a, 7. a, 8. c

Pages 124–125: A. 1. b, 2. a, 3. b, 4. c, 5. a, 6. c, 7. b, 8. b

Page 126: 1. b, 2. d, 3. a, 4. c, 5. b, 6. d, 7. a, 8. c

Page 127: 1. b, 2. a, 3. c, 4. a, 5. d, 6. b, 7. a, 8. b

Pages 132–133: A. 1. b, 2. a, 3. b, 4. b, 5. b, 6. a, 7. a, 8. b; B. 1. sentences, 2. deed, 3. just, 4. admitted

Pages 134–135: A. 1. b, 2. b, 3. a, 4. a, 5. b, 6. a, 7. a, 8. b; B. 1. view, 2. sole, 3. office, 4. term

Pages 136–137: A. 1. b, 2. a, 3. b, 4. b, 5. a, 6. a, 7. b, 8. a; B. 1. composition, 2. fashion, 3. novel, 4. inclined

Page 138: 1. b, 2. c, 3. a, 4. b, 5. c, 6. b, 7. a, 8. b

Page 139: 1. a, 2. c, 3. a, 4. a, 5. b, 6. c

Pages 144–145: A. 1. b, 2. c, 3. b, 4. a, 5. c, 6. a, 7. c, 8. b

Pages 146–147: A. 1. b, 2. a, 3. c, 4. b, 5. a, 6. b, 7. c, 8. a

Page 148: 1. c, 2. b, 3. a, 4. c, 5. d, 6. c

UNIT III STUDY SKILLS

Page 151: 1. c, 2. b, 3. d
Page 153: 1. d, 2. b, 3. b, 4. b, 5. a, 6. b
Page 155: 1. a, 2. c, 3. b, 4. c, 5. b, 6. a
Page 157: 1. b, 2. c, 3. d, 4. a, 5. a, 6. d
Page 159: 1. a, 2. d, 3. b, 4. a, 5. c, 6. b
Page 161: 1. a, 2. a, 3. c, 4. d, 5. c, 6. c
Page 163: 1. a, 2. b, 3. d, 4. d, 5. b, 6. b
Page 165: 1. d, 2. a, 3. c, 4. a, 5. a, 6. d
Page 167: 1. b, 2. d, 3. a, 4. a, 5. c, 6. b
Page 169: 1. b, 2. a, 3. b, 4. b, 5. b, 6. d
Page 171: 1. d, 2. c, 3. b, 4. a, 5. c, 6. a
Page 172: 1. a, 2. a, 3. b, 4. c, 5. b, 6. c
Page 173: 1. c, 2. b, 3. c. 4. d. 5. b, 6. d
Page 175: 1. d, 2. a, 3. c
Page 177: 1. b, 2. d, 3. c, 4. c, 5. d, 6. a
Page 179: 1. c, 2. b, 3. d, 4. c, 5. a, 6. b
Page 181: 1. a, 2. b, 3. d, 4. c, 5. d, 6. b
Page 183: 1. d, 2. a, 3. c, 4. d, 5. d, 6. a
Page 185: 1. c, 2. d, 3. b, 4. b, 5. b, 6. c
Page 187: 1. c, 2. b, 3. c, 4. c, 5. b, 6. a
Page 189: 1. a, 2. d, 3. c, 4. d, 5. b, 6. a
Page 191: 1. c, 2. c, 3. c, 4. a, 5. a, 6. c
Page 193: 1. c, 2. b, 3. d, 4. a, 5. d, 6. c
Page 194: 1. b, 2. c, 3. d, 4. b, 5. a, 6. b, 7. d, 8. b
Page 195: 1. b, 2. a, 3. c, 4. b
Page 196: 1. b, 2. c, 3. c, 4. a, 5. b, 6. c

UNIT IV   TESTS

Test 1

Reading Comprehension (pages 198–201): 1. c, 2. d, 3. c, 4. b, 5. a, 6. b, 7. c, 8. a, 9. c, 10. d, 11. a, 12. d, 13. b, 14. c, 15. d, 16. c, 17. b, 18. a, 19. b, 20. d

Vocabulary (pages 202–204): 1. d, 2. c, 3. b, 4. c, 5. a, 6. b, 7. c, 8. c, 9. b, 10. d, 11. d, 12. b, 13. a, 14. a, 15. b, 16. b, 17. b, 18. b, 19. b, 20. a, 21. a, 22. b

Study Skills (pages 205–207): 1. c, 2. d, 3. a, 4. b, 5. c, 6. a, 7. b, 8. c, 9. a, 10. b, 11. c, 12. c, 13. d, 14. b, 15. b, 16. a, 17. c, 18. a, 19. b, 20. c, 21. a, 22. d, 23. a, 24. c,

Test 2

Reading Comprehension (pages 208–211): 1. b, 2. c, 3. a, 4. c, 5. d, 6. b, 7. d, 8. a, 9. c, 10. b, 11. c, 12. d, 13. a, 14. c, 15. b, 16. b, 17. a, 18. d, 19. c, 20. b

Vocabulary (pages 212–214): 1. c, 2. b, 3. c, 4. a, 5. c, 6. d, 7. b, 8. c, 9. b, 10. c, 11. b, 12. d, 13. a, 14. c, 15. c, 16. a, 17. c, 18. a, 19. d, 20. b, 21. b, 22. d

Study Skills (pages 215–217): 1. a, 2. d, 3. b, 4. a, 5. d, 6. d, 7. c, 8. a, 9. c, 10. a, 11. d, 12. a, 13. d, 14. c, 15. c, 16. b, 17. b, 18. d, 19. c, 20. c, 21. a